THE SYNCHRONICITY CODE

Printed in the United States of America
ISBN-13: 978-1461036975

ISBN-10: 1461036976

Learn more information at:
www.SynchronicityCode.com

.

The Synchronicity Code
How to Follow Coincidence
And (sometimes even)
Predict the Future

The Synchronicity Code presents a new discovery about the way history repeats across hidden cycles of time. The author's experience as an investor based on cycles led to this discovery. As the research progressed, it soon became clear that meaningful coincidences are the key to de-coding the patterns of history.

From wars to assassinations, to inventions to the birth of sages, The Synchronicity Code presents case after case demonstrating the theory in action, at times with such stunning accuracy as to be nearly beyond belief. Most of the examples are drawn from well-known historical events, so anyone can verify them.

Not only does The Synchronicity Code show the links between events of the past, it also offers a way to predict, the timing of events in the future. The Synchronicity Code will teach you how to do the calculations yourself.

Thus begins a new adventure in man's relationship to his own history, as The Synchronicity Code puts a new slant on an old question: Is he who knows history condemned to repeat it?

TABLE OF CONTENTS

"A TRULY AMAZING DISCOVERY. ALTHOUGH I'M NO MATH WHIZ, GOODMAN HAS PUT HIS THEORY TOGETHER STEP BY STEP WITH CLARITY AND EXCITING DETAIL. DISCOVER YOUR OWN NUMERIC HISTORY. BUT DON'T MISS THIS FAR-OUT READ!"

Patty de Llosa, author of THE PRACTICE OF PRESENCE and TAMING YOUR INNER TYRANT.

"I have just completed the section regarding Christ/Mohammed/Buddha, and all I can say is that I AM THOROUGHLY IMPRESSED, INTRIGUED and, yes, STUNNED by your efforts! Also, I feel extremely honored that you have shared this with me. I just had to pause and let you know that." Len Vinci

"Mr. Goodman has uncovered and meticulously documented an incredible mathematical theory about how history repeats that demands the attention of our larger academic community. His assertion is tantalizingly bold, and if found to withstand more rigorous scrutiny, will expand our understanding of the universe - and our place in it - exponentially. It is a fascinating piece of work." Matthew J. Bijur

"If your book about Fibonacci and other ratios predicting historical events were a work of fiction, it would be provocative and intriguing. But for real? If this turns out to be true (and you give strong evidence that it is), then I don't even know what to think about it. History will never be viewed the same way it was before you shared your discovery." Jack G. Zurlini, Jr.

i

To Martha, Sam, Tess and Sadie

PREFACE

First, a very warm thanks to my brother Greg, sister Lauren, Patty Llosa, Nicole Ferrante, Jack Lee, Paul Gubitosa, Dawn Goldberg, Pete Dama, Sarah Tanner and my wife Martha, for their generous support and assistance in this project.

Revealing the Synchronicity Code raises philosophical and moral questions for me. After much deliberation, I have concluded that now is the time to come forward with this unique material.

I do not believe that events are predetermined. Consequently, I do not believe that events must *necessarily* unfold according to any specific timeframe under the Synchronicity Code. However, if they must occur, I believe that the magnitude of adverse events can be lessened by knowing, in advance, that a key event is foretold.

My purpose in writing this book is so that knowledge of the Synchronicity Code can be used as a force for good.

May it be so for you.

1

INTRODUCTION

To every thing there is a season, and a time to every purpose under the heaven.   Ecclesiastes 3:1

A NEW DISCOVERY ABOUT HOW HISTORY REPEATS

This book is being readied for publication near the 10-year anniversary of the day when planes crashed into the World Trade Center and the Pentagon on September 11, 2001. This horrific attack was a defining moment in the history of America, similar to the Japanese attack on Pearl Harbor sixty years earlier.

What is not widely known about 9/11 is that its connection to Pearl Harbor is not just an idea thought up by a news analyst. *Pearl Harbor is mathematically connected to 9/11 by a "surprise attack cycle" that is accurate to within one day.* That cycle also involved the first bombing on the World Trade Center on February 26, 1993, when a van parked below the North Tower exploded, killing 6 and injuring over a thousand people.

It seems impossible that this should be true. When adjusted based on the time of day of the events, just over 3118 days (roughly 8.5 years) separates the first World Trade Center bombing and 9/11. If you take that precise interval and "roll it back" from 9/11 seven times, through 1984, 1976, 1967, 1958 and 1950, you hit 1941. But not just 1941. You hit December, 1941. But not just December 1941. You hit *December 7, 1941—the exact day of the Pearl Harbor attack.*

This mathematical coincidence is certainly incredible. But it is not unique. *All major historical events of the last century also exhibit a similar type of ordering across time.*

Pearl Harbor and 9/11, the 1929 Crash, the assassination in Sarajevo that triggered World War 1, Germany's invasion of Poland in 1939, the Cuban Missile Crisis, the assassination of John F. Kennedy, the nuclear arms race, stock market crashes, the Oklahoma City bombing, the sinking of the Titanic, even the killing of Osama bin Laden: these events are etched in our consciousness as among the most stirring events over the last hundred years. Each one of them is also precisely timed, based on a heretofore unknown numeric cycle, or code.

And this same mathematical formula or code holds true hundreds, even thousands of years in the past. The invention of the telephone, the phonograph, and the light bulb, the signing of the Declaration of Independence, the crowning of Charlemagne, the Napoleonic Wars, Joan of Arc, the Norman Conquest, the birth of Christ, the Buddha, and Mohammed: each of these were also accurately mapped across time by an unknown code that I will show you.

Common expressions such as "history repeats" and "things happen in threes" hint at the underlying phenomenon that the Synchronicity Code makes explicit. The Synchronicity Code takes this out of the realm of generalities and shows it to be based on a hidden mathematical order. What repeats is not the exact incident over and over. But the *meaning* is repeated in subsequent events, linked by simple divisions of time.

This code is active not just in the major events of history. It is active in the personal events of individuals as they go about their day to day lives. It gives new insight into events that occurred in the past, and a method to predict what may happen in the future. For example, over a year in advance, the author was aware that the surprise attack cycle predicted a future incident on or about March 27, 2010. *This turned out to be within one day of North Korea's torpedo attack on South Korea!*

* * *

It has been quipped that "history does not unfold: it piles up"[1].

I say history doesn't pile up. It rolls.

This is a new discovery about the way seemingly random events unfold across time. Things don't just happen when they happen. They happen when they're *supposed* to happen.

What determines when events are supposed to happen?

It is the *interval of time* between two events that determines when a subsequent event will occur. It all boils down to hidden cycles, but to see them, we need to calculate simple fractions between the two outside events, such as 1/2, 1/3, 1/4, in order to arrive at them. These intervals then "roll" forward to find the next related event in the sequence.

Put succinctly, historical events are numerically correlated across time with other meaningfully-related historical events. This shouldn't be happening if the timing of events is entirely random, as is usually presupposed. This means that a heretofore unrecognized force is choreographing the actions of millions upon millions of people. I will show evidence of this in past events. Yet this same unknown force is at work behind

---

[1] Quote by Robert M. Adams

the scenes *right now*, choreographing future events out of what has occurred in the recent and more distant past.

How do events relate according to the Synchronicity Code?

They relate *meaningfully*.

What this means is that events of a given theme or meaning are linked together. War links to war; inventions to inventions, and the lives of great sages are linked to the lives of other great sages, sometimes across great spans of time.

The way this works is often (but not always) straight forward. Take two thematically related events, especially ones involving *meaningful coincidences*. For example, let's say that you and your sister were born 3 years apart on almost the exact same calendar day—one on February 18th and the other on February 19th. That's the type of coincidence we would be interested in. Then "roll forward" the interval of time between these two birthdates by three years, six years, nine years, each a multiple of the initial three-year duration, and look for a related event to occur at that later date: perhaps the birth (or death) of another family member or some other event of significance to you and your sister.

Sometimes the measured duration is as simple as 1 + 1 + 1. Sometimes it is hidden until the occurrence of the third event, and the pattern is revealed by "rolling backwards" to the first event of the series. That's how I found the Surprise Attack Cycle. One important cycle is based on the ancient Greeks' "Golden Section," which is the key mathematical proportion used in the Parthenon. Since the middle ages, this proportion is also known as the Fibonacci ratio. We'll show how this works later, but a very clear and important case of the Synchronicity Code uses the Golden Section in a time sequence that links the beginnings of the Revolutionary War, the Civil War and World War I accurately across 139 years.

I call this phenomenon the *Synchronicity Code* because (i) the mathematical correlation of events across time is an expression of synchronicity (a meaningful coincidence), in the numeric relationship itself, and (ii) significant cases of this phenomenon are often accompanied by parallel meaningful coincidences; the case of Lincoln and Kennedy, discussed in Chapter 8, is a prime example of this.

Isn't "Synchronicity Code" just a fancy term for "cycle?" you might ask.

Yes. But there are differences between the Synchronicity Code and natural cycles. The differences are:

1. **Not always a regular periods**. The term "cycle" usually applies to events with fixed recurring periods. Regular periodicity also occurs in the Synchronicity Code, but not always. For example, when the time sequence expresses via the Fibonacci ratio, there is a logarithmic increase or decrease as the progression proceeds, which is geometrically

depicted as a spiral. This is not like a typical periodic cycle.

2. **Whole number divisions and multiples**. Unlike a regular cycle, the Synchronicity Code sequence expresses anywhere along a series of whole number fractions (1/4, 1/3, 1/2, etc.). It is possible to have a Synchronicity Code correlation at both the 1/4 and 2/3 points (which I call "TimeMarks" or just "Marks") in one series.

3. **Acausal.** For most cycles there is a known or presumed cause for the cycle, such as the movement of the tides or the cycle of the seasons. There is no known cause for the Synchronicity Code.[2]

4. **Synchronicity.** The Synchronicity Code is of course related to the phenomenon of meaningful coincidences, or to use the term coined by C.G. Jung, *synchronicity*. You may find correlations between events that don't exhibit synchronicity per se. But your odds of finding a "hit" are higher if you measure off of two events that are synchronously related.

5. **The Power of Ten.** The *magnitude* of an event in a Synchronicity Code series often appears to be related to timeframes ending in "zero": 10 (20, 30, 40 etc.) years, 100 years, 1000 years. As we will see later, this may be one of the

---

[2] The ancient Greeks hypothesized that number itself was causal, but this principle has yet to be approached by modern science.

reasons why the 9/11 attacks were so devastating.

6.   **Precise Correlations.** It would not be expected for a natural cycle on the scale of years to express itself with pinpoint accuracy on the scale of days.   Yet this happens with the Synchronicity Code over and over, and when it does, it is one of the strongest reasons to believe that the discovery is real.

7.   **Focus on human beings.** The focus of the Synchronicity Code is on events which have a significant *cognitive meaning for human beings.* We are looking for the Synchronicity Code in the recorded history of mankind (as well as the personal unrecorded history of individual lives), not in scientific data related to, say, species on the Galapagos Islands.

* * *

Do *all* human events relate by means of the Synchronicity Code?

That is somewhat hard to answer. Not all events will show simple and obvious time correlations.   Yet I will show centuries-long correlations of major events affecting much of civilization, which suggests that a broad principle is at work, choreographing the actions of huge masses of people.

For a relatively small group of traders and investors who research number-based cycles in the markets, this will already be of second-nature. In trading, the use of cycles is all about predicting. That's true here too; Chapter 12 is devoted to predictions of future events. But even if prediction were not possible, the fact that the main events of history have been invisibly orchestrated in this way, should come as a revelation.

Most of the examples in this book are based on well-known historical events, so the dates are readily verifiable. I encourage you to check the calculations. Historians will now have a new sub-field to research, consisting of the comparative analysis of events along a Code timeline. Coincidences can be plumbed for intent; for example, were conspiracies involved in the first two assassinations? Look for a conspiracy in the third.

The Synchronicity Code also applies to your personal life. Up until this point you have likely assumed that there is little rhyme or reason to *when* things happen to you. Your life may seem to follow a general plan that at some point (more often than not) includes some version of career, marriage, children. Some of this is mapped out in a linear fashion by virtue of the natural process of growing up to adulthood. But why did you meet your partner just *now*? Why did that accident change the course of your life just *then*? The Synchronicity Code suggests these things are not as random as you may have thought.

The *when* is important to know, because it informs the *why* of your life. By this I mean that if a time sequence marks a specific *when* that puts three (or more) events in mathematical relationship, then you have your finger on the pulse of why. There is a story to tell whenever events line up via the Synchronicity Code.

For example, the Synchronicity Code suggests that the key story of the life of George Washington, *for him,* centers on his career as a *warrior,* as the Commander in Chief. Not just of the Continental Army during the Revolutionary War, but in the French and Indian War, where he was *also* Commander in Chief of His Majesty's colony, Virginia. We will show this timeline in Chapter 6.

Washington crossing the Delaware by Emmanuel Leutze

This book is premised on the notion that meaningful coincidences (time-related or otherwise) are not all just plain old chance. Some readers will struggle with the thesis simply because they can't rationally fathom how it possibly could be true. I am sympathetic to a point. Yet some things transcend ordinary reason. The challenge remains to squarely face the evidence that is presented, for it offers the opportunity to embrace a brand new way of looking at things.

1

THE COMPASS OF TIME

Numbers rule the Universe. Pythagoras

The ancient Greeks were right. Everything *is* arranged according to number. But until now no one has shown how this truth applies to events as they unfold across time. No one has even hypothesized that events, possibly *all* events, are linked together by hidden cycles of time, which cycles are marked by meaningful coincidences.

Until now.

A Crowning Point

It was a really good day. The pomp and ceremony included dozens of processions, of cardinals, grand officers, and the imperial cavalcade. The royal coach, embossed in gold and displaying the capital letter "N", was pulled by eight horses up to Notre Dame cathedral. Imperial regalia of scepter, sword, crown and red coronation robes reminiscent of Charlemagne adorned the event. Josephine took her place on a smaller throne five steps below. Pope Pius VII had been brought up from Rome to perform the ceremony. But at just the right moment, Napoleon brushed the Pope aside, grasped the crown and placed it on his own head. The coronation had been so well orchestrated, it is hard to imagine that Napoleon hadn't planned to crown himself from the start.

The ceremonial reminiscences to Charlemagne are more than just happenstance. The crowning of Napoleon happened very near to 1000 years after Charlemagne declared himself emperor in 800 AD. This millennial time span, together with other synchronous time parallels, suggests that the Synchronicity Code was at work behind the scenes. The parallels include several key events in each ruler's life. Charlemagne's reign began in 768. A thousand years later (+1), Napoleon was born in 1769. Charlemagne's rule ended upon his death in 814,

Napoleon's rule ended upon his defeat in Waterloo in 1815, again, a thousand years (+1) later.[3]

Next, we will take the coincidence-rich pairing of Charlemagne and Napoleon and apply the Code sequence. To do this we simply divide the 1000-year time span by the most obvious fractions, 1/4, 1/3, 1/2, etc. (we also include the Fibonacci divisions at .382 and .618) and add those numbers to the year 814. However, we would not expect to find a meaningfully-related event at each of these divisions. Even one strong hit would be notable. Here there are several.

What we discover is that a major event involving a French conqueror took place almost exactly at the 1/4 Mark. In September of the year 1066, a mere 2 years from the exact Mark (which is quite precise given the thousand year time span), William the Conqueror successfully led the Norman Conquest of England, replacing the native Scandinavian ruling class with a French-speaking monarchy. Here again, we find parallel milestone dates, this time mapping major events in the reigns of *all three rulers* which evidence the behind-the-scenes workings of the Code. To find these, transpose William's dates forward by 750 years to track Napoleon, or backwards by 250 years to track Charlemagne. William first secured control of Normandy in 1547. When translated backwards to 797, this marked an important victory for Charlemagne against Barcelona, at

---

[3] I would argue that Napoleon's reign really ended upon Napoleon's first abdication in April of 1814 following his defeat in the Battle of Leipzig and the subsequent invasion of France by Coalition forces. This would synchronize the end of each ruler's reign to exactly 1000 years.

that time one of the greatest cities in Moor-controlled southern Europe. When translated forward to 1797, it marked the successful conclusion of Napoleon's first campaign at the helm of the French army in the signing of the Treaty of Leoben. In 1554, William successfully rebuffed an invasion by King Henry I of France, securing his hegemony as Duke of Normandy. When translated back to 804, this marked the year when several Italian territories finally came under Charlemagne's control, and when translated forward to 1804, this is the year Napoleon crowned himself emperor.

Charlemagne, William and Napoleon are the three most prominent military conquerors in the history of France. Some would argue that Clovis (c. 466-511) should be added to this list. This is perfectly in line with the Synchronicity Code. Clovis began his rule in 481 AD, which is *exactly* 333 years (1/3 of the Charlemagne-Napoleon line) prior to the death of Charlemagne.

There is yet another famous French military leader whose appearance is precisely marked on the same Code timeline. The .618 (Fibonacci ratio) Mark hits the year 1432. This is within one year of the death of Joan of Arc, thus ending her brief but brilliant three year military sojourn. From the moment she arrived at the siege of Orléans in April, 1429 until her capture in May of 1430 (finally ending with her being burned at the stake in 1431), Joan of Arc accomplished a string of stunning victories believed by many to be divinely inspired. These victories reversed the downward spiral of France during the Hundred Years War and led to the coronation of Charles VII. It is quite fitting then that, centuries later,

Napoleon was the first to use Joan of Arc as a political symbol in support of his rule. She came from the same (Synchronicity Code) line!

Finally, the 1/3 Mark up from the death of Charlemagne, in 1147, hits the exact moment when Louis VII of France embarked on the Second Crusade. This is significant not because Louis was a great military leader (he wasn't), but because this was the first Crusade in which a European king led his armies into battle. By exact, we mean *exact*. Charlemagne died in January of 814, and Napoleon's defeat at Waterloo was in June of 1815. Louis embarked in June of 1147, which would have been only two or three months from the exact 1/3 Mark, depending on whether you use Waterloo or Napoleon's abdication as the end date. This level of precision over the vast millennial time span is remarkable.

The following summarizes the Synchronicity Code hits over the 1000-year period:

The Charlemagne—Napoleon Timeline

- Pre-1000 year span – 1/3 Mark: 481 AD **Clovis begins his reign.**
-
- 814 AD **End of Charlemagne's reign upon his death.**
-
- 1/4 Mark: 1066 AD **William the Conqueror successfully leads the Norman Conquest of**

England, begins reign as Norman King of England (*exact: 1064 AD*).

-
- 1/3 Mark: 1147 AD **Louis VII of France embarks on the Second Crusade** (*exact:1047 AD—a precise hit*).

-
- .618 Mark: 1431 AD **Joan of Arc is burned at the stake** (*exact:1432 AD*).

-
- 1815 AD **Napoleon's reign ends in his defeat at Waterloo.**

Question: 1/4, 1/3, .618, why should we care about these time divisions at all? Because this is the way the "time cycles" of history manifest. It is not always as simple as rolling a particular fixed time duration forward (although sometimes it is that simple). Instead, the cycles are akin to "vibrations," that unfold according to basic whole number divisions. In short, the interval between two related events marks future events based on these fractional divisions. If you know this, then you can begin to anticipate and predict when a future event might occur.

Question: Aren't you mixing and matching a bit here? Joan of Arc was not a king. And Louis VII was not a major conqueror. This depends in part on how you characterize the meaning of the timeline. If you characterize the line as "major events involving the most famous French military leaders of all time", then Joan of Arc belongs. If the line is "major events in French military history", then Louis' Second Crusade would likely belong as well. But even if Joan and Louis were dropped out, the line still stands with Clovis, Charlemagne, William and Napoleon.

We will return to the Napoleonic era as we examine other major events that shaped modern history. In particular, the abdication of Napoleon in 1814 following his defeat at Leipzig, is a pivotal juncture from which future Synchronicity Code sequences continue to unfold.

* * *

The next series of cases is unprecedented in terms of its rich complexity and precision.

The Kennedy Curse

The Kennedy Curse refers to the unusually high number of tragedies that have befallen the wealthy, politically prominent Kennedy family since the 1940s. In researching this case, there are so many tragic incidents that one can easily get lost. So it is important to begin, not at the beginning, but with coincidences, in the form of date similarities, such as dates clustering at the end of November over various years. From there it is possible to unravel the sequencing of events in a manner that accounts for many of the unfortunate events that happened along the way. What's interesting about the Kennedy case is that more than one series rolls forward based on fixed cycles of either 5 or 6 years.

From the list of Kennedy misfortunes, the closest thing to a coincidence lies in the pair of dates involving the Chappaquiddick incident occurring on July 18, 1969, and the July 16, 1999 plane crash that killed John F. Kennedy, Jr. along with his wife and sister in law. The dates are almost exactly 30 years apart, which for our purposes constitutes a number coincidence; so that is the base for our measurements.

30 years can be divided into the whole number parts of either 3 x 10 years or 5 x 6 years. Each of these smaller numbers could cycle or "roll out" from the initial event and also hit the 30 year mark. Here, the 5-year interval captures Chappaquiddick, all plane crash incidents except for the Cavendish plane crash, and more. As you review the events, notice that most of the hits fall within about a month of the July base dates, thus making it fairly accurate over a 55 year time span.

The 5-year Kennedy cycle

August 12, 1944 Joseph P. Kennedy, Jr. is killed in a mid-air explosion during a mission in World War II.

[1949, 1954, 1959] No publicly known event.

4 x 5 = June 19, 1964 Senator Ted Kennedy is in a plane crash in which one of his aides and the pilot are killed.

5 x 5 = July 18, 1969 Chappaquiddick incident: a car driven by Ted Kennedy goes off a bridge in Martha's Vineyard, resulting in the drowning of Mary Jo Kopechne.

[1974, 1979] No publicly known event.

8 x 5 = April 25, 1984 David Anthony Kennedy dies from a drug overdose.

[1989, 1994] No publicly known event.[4]

10 x 5 = July 16, 1999 John F. Kennedy, Jr. and others are killed in plane crash.

[2004] No publicly known event.

12 x 5 = August 25, 2009 Edward M. ("Ted") Kennedy dies of brain tumor.

I do not consider it a "miss" that an event does not occur at *each* 5-year increment. While sometimes the Synchronicity Code will hit every Mark, in general that is not the way this type of cycle tends to manifest.

The 6-year Kennedy cycle

In this next series, the Synchronicity Code "jumps" to a high level of precision, where the Marks fall far more precisely than would seem possible. This is where the odds against the Synchronicity Code being pure chance really begin to pile up.[5] The timeline begins with the fact that Caroline Kennedy and her brother John

---

[4] Arguably, Jacqueline Kennedy's death at the relatively age of 65 on May 19, 1994 would constitute an event for inclusion on the timeline.

[5] At synchronicitycode.com, you can contribute your own discoveries to the database of the strongest, most extraordinary cases.

F. Kennedy, Jr. were both born at the tail end of November almost exactly 3 years apart. That is our starting coincidental pair. This time span then rolls forward once and hits the death of their father, President John F. Kennedy, at the 6-year Mark. It shows a mathematically precise cycle between the 1957, 1960 and 1963 events.

Jacqueline Kennedy, Robert Kennedy, John Jr, Caroline and Peter Lawford at the funeral of John Fitzgerald Kennedy, November 25, 1963

Births and death

- Caroline Kennedy born November 27, 1957
-
-

- 1/2 Mark: JFK, Jr. born November 25, 1960
-
-
- President Kennedy dies November 22, 1963

The total number of days elapsed is 2186, which is almost exactly 6 years. The precise date for the 50% Mark, corresponding to JFK, Jr.'s birth, would be November 24, 1960, *within a mere day*. We would have to analyze the exact hours in which these events occurred to know if it is actually within a one day tolerance. But regardless, this is incredibly precise.

Again note the calendar dates of November 27, November 25 and November 22; they are very close together. It is not uncommon for anniversary dates to synchronize in this fashion, adding to the list of supporting coincidences that reveals the workings of the Synchronicity Code.

Was this pure chance?

I don't think so. If it were pure chance, *then Joseph Kennedy, Sr., JFK's father, would not have died on the same cycle rolled out to November 18, 1969.* Again, note the November date. The precision of this sequence is stunning.

This kind of thing would mean nothing if it was a one-off coincidence. Leaving aside the fact that this book is filled with similar date and time related coincidences, realize that we *started* with the coincidental calendar dates of Carolyn and JFK, Jr.'s birthdates and *looked for* the further coincidence that we found: a major event in November of 1963. Then, the fact that Joseph Kennedy Sr.'s death *also* fit so precisely to that same sequence simply *corroborates the theory.* The odds of this correlation happening by accident seem beyond chance, but in a way they *are* chance.

The Synchronicity Code is the unseen architecture of chance.

While history does not "pile up" (it rolls), the Synchronicity Code piles up example after example of a hidden sequencing of events that defies the odds. It seems rather unbelievable even to me, but the foregoing timeline continues. JFK, Jr. *also died on the same sequence* on July 16, 1999, now spanning a total of 42 years. This makes it "like father like son" … like grandson.[6]

Where this extended timeline is slightly at variance is that the date of death for JFK, Jr. does not synchronize with the November calendar dates from the original timeline. But sometimes there is simply *too much history* being choreographed at one time for every date to match precisely. Recall that the death of JFK, Jr. synchronizes almost exactly (within 2 days) with Teddy Kennedy's Chappaquiddick incident, and this coincidence was the basis for unraveling the 5-year cycle with which we began. Also, Jackie Kennedy was born on July 28, 1929. The birth of the mother and death of the

---

[6] The cycles shown in the Kennedy case study may continue into the future. Chapter 12 Predicting the Future is devoted to exploring events that have yet to occur.

son are connected by almost exactly 70 years, which is an expression of the Power of Ten, the importance of which is discussed in Chapter 4.

We could go on and on. Tragic as it was, it could be argued that Teddy Kennedy got off easy in the Chappaquiddick incident. It occurred within one week of the 1.25 Mark taking as the base dates the assassinations of John F. Kennedy on November 22, 1963 and Robert F. Kennedy on June 6, 1968.

"Ok. Pretty interesting. But anyone could find dates to prove anything, if you look hard enough."

Perhaps. But we didn't have to look hard. We took a couple of obvious base measuring dates (obvious because of their similar calendar dates) to see if there were any time-related synchronicities and found a number of them that were far more accurate than we could have anticipated. I agree, it is hard to know what to make of it, but the fact is that precise, cyclical time matrixes underlie the lives of the Kennedy's. I am sure there is much more to be found, too. We have barely dipped our toes in the water and already we are swimming in time-related coincidences.

* * *

The Synchronicity Code weaves Inventions

To fill the hour—that is happiness. Ralph Waldo Emerson

I have been a huge fan of Thomas Alva Edison since I was a young boy. To me, invention is happiness.

As I have already suggested, the way to decipher the Synchronicity Code is to "follow the coincidences," because coincidences are (for some reason) integral to how history repeats across time. Both Thomas Edison and Alexander Graham Bell were born in 1847, on February 11th and March 3rd, respectively (about three weeks apart). Ha! I think. I bet these famous inventors have interconnected Synchronicity Code timelines involving their main inventions.

They do.

Bell's patent for the telephone was granted on March 7, 1876. 1421 days later, on January 27, 1880, Edison was granted his patent for the incandescent light. In between, on February 19, 1878, Edison patented his phonograph. This middle date falls *within three days* of the precise 1/2 Mark between these seminal inventions:

Edison and Bell

- **Telephone** patented March 7, 1876
-
- 1/2 Mark: **Phonograph** patented February 19, 1878 (*exact: February 16, 1878*)
-
- **Light Bulb** patented January 27, 1880

While the telephone is what Alexander Graham Bell is most famous for, Bell personally considered his "photophone", which transmits sound on a beam of light, to be his greatest invention. He was granted a patent for this invention on February 19, 1880. Wait. Didn't we just see that calendar date? Yes—exactly two years earlier Edison patented his phonograph on February 19th. The names "photophone" and "phonograph" even resemble each other. The two inventors no doubt admired each others work, for on January 25, 1881, close to the 1.5 Mark up from the phonograph and light bulb patent dates, Edison and Bell formed the Oriental Telephone Company to sell telephones in India, Japan, China and other countries. Bell also undertook to improve upon Edison's phonograph and his work made the invention commercially viable.

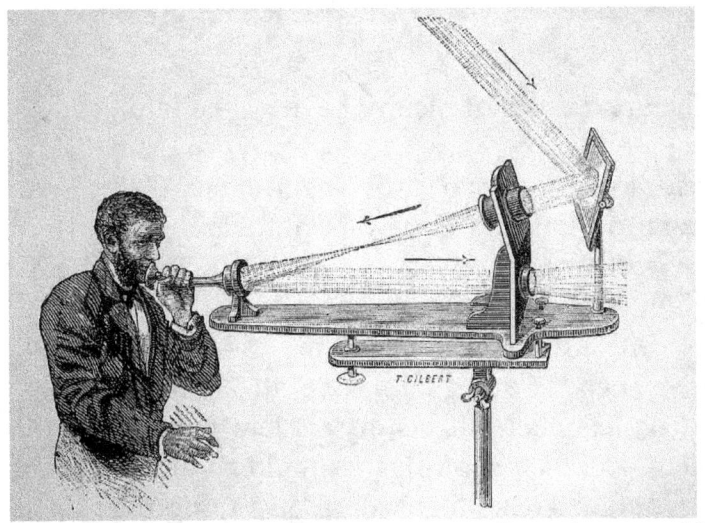

Illustration of photophone's transmitter, invented by Alexander Graham Bell

Thus we find that these two seminal inventors of the industrial revolution were born nearly at the same time and obtained their greatest patents on dates that were integrally woven together via coincidental dates and Synchronicity Code timelines. Prior to the advent of this discovery, if one came across even a small slice of these coincidences, one would simply marvel at it and think, "how odd". Now we see that in fact something more is going on, that the coincidences *mean something*. They mean that events are being mapped across time.

* * *

The Great Sages

Today, be aware of how you are spending your 1,440 beautiful moments, and spend them wisely.   Author Unknown

The great sages of history have gotten into the act.

Prior to discovery of the Synchronicity Code, I had little reason to think the ideas of Confucius were related to the Greek philosophers. Yet even a cursory examination reveals strong parallels between the teachings of Confucius and the ancient Greeks. Confucius, Socrates and Plato were all among the most respected philosophers in history. Plato taught that the wisest men—philosopher kings—should be the leaders of society. Confucius also focused on governing rulers. To him, the best kind of leader was one with impeccable moral character.

Consider the sayings of these great masters:

"When you know a thing, to hold that you know it; and when you do not know a thing, to allow that you do not know it—this is knowledge." Confucius, Analects, 2:17

"I know nothing except the fact of my ignorance." Socrates, from Diogenes Laertius bk.2, sec. 25

"False words are not only evil in themselves, but they infect the soul with evil". Plato, Phaedo.

"Without knowing the force of words, it is impossible to know men." Confucius, Analects, bk. 20.3, iii.

"The man who in the view of gain thinks of righteousness; who in the view of danger is prepared to give up his life; and who does not forget an old agreement however far back it extends—such a man may be reckoned a complete man." Confucius 14:21

"Give me beauty in the inward soul, and may the outward and inward man be at one. May I reckon the wise to be wealthy, and may I have such a quantity of gold as none but the temperate can carry. Dialogues, Phaedrus.

Given the thematic similarities in the teachings of these masters, it is not surprising that the Synchronicity Code should mathematically link up their births. Confucius was born in 551 BC, Socrates in 469 BC and Plato, 428 BC. The number of years between the birthdates of Confucius and Plato is 551-428 = 123. The date of Socrates' birth falls right on the 2/3 Mark between Confucius and Plato: 123/3 = 41. 428 - 41 = 469 BC.

Birthdates: Confucius – Socrates – Plato

- 551 BC **Confucius** is born
-
-
- **2/3 Mark**:   469 BC **Socrates** is born
-
- 428 BC **Plato** is born

Buddha, Pythagoras, Christ, Mohammed

Even more striking than the Confucius-Socrates-Plato timeline is the timeline involving the birthdates of the founders of Christianity, Buddhism and Islam. Surely someone has noticed before that both the Buddha and Pythagoras, two of history's greatest sages, were *both* born on or very close to 570 BC. That alone is a remarkable coincidence. From there the Synchronicity Code reaches *more than a thousand years* across the centuries to the birth of Mohammed in 571 A.D. How strange it is that the number 570 (+1) is repeated, first as a B.C. date, then as an A.D. date. Lest you be concerned that this is some trick of our calendar system, the Anno Domini dating system was established in 525 A.D., *before* the birth of Mohammed, so the implementation of the system could not possibly have taken the birthdates of these sages into account. Further, while any number of calendar dating systems are possible, the Anno Domini system *is the one we happen to live by*. Since the Synchronicity Code correlates events by their meaning, it makes sense that the correlations would make use of the very dating system that means the most to us.

This was meant to be seen.

The key link in this timeline, however, has not yet been stated. It lies in the middle, at the 50% Mark between 570 B.C. and 571 A.D. Of course, this falls right at the cusp between B.C. and A.D., when it is widely believed that Jesus Christ was born. Herod the Great died just a few months after the slaughter of children at Bethlehem (it is said Herod was killed by divine vengeance). Jesus would not have been more than three or four months old at the time. This puts Jesus' birth sometime around 4 BC. That's extremely close to the half way, 50% Mark between 570 BC and 571 AD. Only this time we are spanning more than eleven hundred years, and *miss the exact midpoint by a mere year or two, if at all.* As there is some slight uncertainty about these birth dates, the birth of Christ could in fact fall exactly on the Mark. In any case, given the scale, the middle Mark *cannot not* be considered precise.

Birthdates: Buddha/Pythagoras - Jesus Christ - Mohammed

- Circa 570 BC <u>Both</u> **the Buddha and Pythagoras** are born
-
- 1/2 Mark: Circa 4 BC **Jesus Christ** is born
-
- Circa 571 AD **Mohammed** is born

Think about this for a moment. The Buddha. Christ. Mohammed. It is not possible to name three more influential religious leaders in the last two thousand years. Yet a school child can see it: the births of these sages are precisely linked across a massive span of time by the Synchronicity Code. If nothing else, this timeline speaks loudly for a missing religious tolerance, and for recognition that, as the Dalai Llama has expressed, all religions point to the same goal. Later on we will see that this great line of enlightened sages continues.

One starts to trust the Synchronicity Code when you see things line up like this time after time. If all these correlations happen by pure chance, then pure chance has been very busy.

Still, one can explain away *any* apparent coincidence, no matter how striking, as falling within the bell curve of randomness. To be fair, just because something *could* be mere chance doesn't mean that it is.

In the next chapter, I show you how to do the Synchronicity Code calculations yourself.

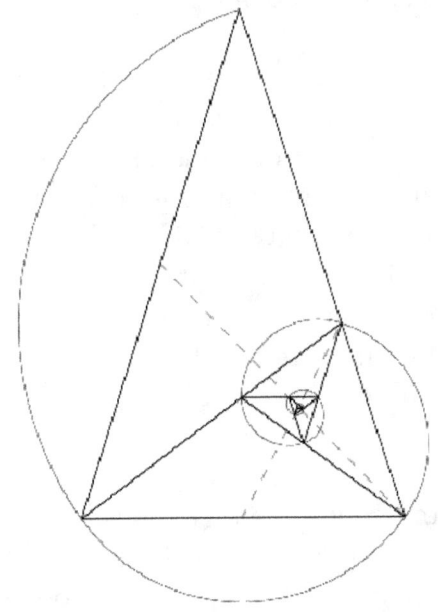

2

JUST MARKING TIME:
HOW TO DO
THE SYNCHRONICITY CODE
CALCULATION

*Do not be troubled by your difficulties with mathematics,
I can assure you mine are much greater.* Albert Einstein

Events unfold according to a mathematical code,
starting from two points in time selected by you. The

timescale could be hours, days, weeks, months, or years. I will give you the calculations so you can test it yourself.

You are born on a certain date. After a certain number of years a significant event happens to you. You get married. Become CEO of a major corporation. Move to the house of your dreams. The duration of time between the date you were born and the day of such significant event can be checked for a future date of a *meaningfully related* third event, at a precise time. Your wedding date, the birth date of a child, the date of a spouse's death—these are all dates to look at to find correlations.

Here's how you do the calculation. (If you freeze up at the mere suggestion of doing any math whatsoever, don't worry. We'll do the calculations for you. Just look at the big picture.)[7]

1.   Pick two dates that you want to research: the birth and death dates of a family member, your own birth date and the date you were married or when a child was born, or perhaps two dates when you had major career changes. If two dates involve a coincidence of some kind, that's ideal. Otherwise, pick two dates that seem to you to be meaningfully related to one another. Experiment. You can start with two major dates in a person's life and look for time connections that allow you to "back into" the underlying meaning, which can be unexpected, should the Synchronicity Code show a connection.

---

[7] At synchronicitycode.com there is a calculator that allows you to calculate Synchronicity Code Marks just by inserting two starting dates.

2.   Count the number of days between these dates.[8] Divide this duration into:
>   (i) .33 (one-third),
>   (ii) .382 (inverse Fibonacci ratio),
>   (iii) .5 (half),
>   (iv) .618 (Fibonacci ratio), and
>   (v) .66 (two-thirds).

(A few other logical divisions are possible, as shown in the examples in this book.)

These divisions will be referred to as TimeMarks, or simply "Marks". Now put the Marks on a timeline and see if any significant milestones line up, depending on the scale of time involved, within +/- one year, one month, one week or even within one day.

It's as simple as that!

A mathematician is someone who can take a cup of coffee and turn it into a theory. Paul Erdos

Example. My father was born in 1929 and died in 2007. We'll take these as the two outside dates and look for significant events occurring at whole number fractions between those dates.

2007-1929 =78.

---

[8] I usually start by counting years, and if there is a hit on the yearly scale, I will then re-do the calculation using the SynchronicityCode.com calculator on the daily scale to determine the precise Mark.

(i) .33 (one-third): 78 x .33 = 26 years
(ii) .382 (inverse Fibonacci ratio): 78 x .382 = 30 years
(iii) .5 (half): 78 x .5 = 39 years
(iv) .618 (Fibonacci ratio): 78 x 48 years
(v) .66 (two-thirds): 78 x .66 = 51 years

Now let's see what happened at these Marks.

1929 + 26 = 1955: My parents were married in the second half of 1954, close to the 1/3 Mark.

1929 + 30 = 1959: At this TimeMark, my parents moved into the home they would live in for most of their lives and I was born within less than two months from the exact Mark.

1929 + 39=1968: Around this time, my father's law practice becomes successful. Now I don't have an exact date for this, and probably wouldn't include this if I were doing a rigorous study. But if I were studying someone's life like my father's, I would be looking for a career change or development at a Mark.

1929 + 51 = 1980: My father was an avid runner and he fulfilled a lifelong desire on this Mark: he ran in the New York City Marathon, which he only did once. This one too seems more anecdotal than, say, my parent's wedding or the move into their lifelong home. But I do think it was really important to my father.

Timeline of Lawrence G. Goodman

- **Born** 1929
-
- .33 1955 Marries my mother
-
- .382 1959 Moves to lifelong home; I am born (*This was also 30 years...Power of Ten—see Chapter 5*)
-
- .5 Circa 1968 Career as attorney takes off.
-
- .66 Achieves long-term goal of running in the NYC Marathon
-
- **Dies** 2007

Questions and Answers

1. *Why do you use .33, .382, .5, 618, and .66? Aren't there many possible fractions?* You are free to experiment with other fractions, and it can be useful to do so when looking at events close to the beginning and end of a person's life, where I would include .25 and .75 Marks, as well as .2 and .8 Marks. But the logic is based on simple math. Take one whole. Cut it <u>once</u> in half—that's of course the ½ Mark. Cut it in half again—that's the ¼ and ¾ Marks. Cut the one whole <u>twice</u> into three equal parts, those Marks are 1/3 and 2/3rds.

2. *What about .382 and .618?* These Marks are based on the Fibonacci number sequence, a very special series of numbers that are a natural growth progression found in nature and which was revered by the great priest-architects of antiquity. The Fibonacci ratio (also known as the Golden Ratio or the Golden Section) is integral to the design of the Greek Parthenon, the Pyramids of Giza and other seminal structures from ancient times. Many Wall Street traders believe, as I do, that the ratio figures prominently in the movement of stock and commodity prices, perhaps for the same reason that the Fibonacci ratio expresses itself in nature. While the ratio is somewhat unique compared to the other divisions, at times it is crucial, such as the Revolutionary War—Civil War—World War I timeline discussed in Chapter 9, which is quite precise over 139 years.

3. *What is the margin for error that you use?* In the above example, the margin for error is plus or minus one year.

4. *With such a margin for error, doesn't that allow for a lot of hits?* Yes. The yearly timeframe, in this first example, is the least refined application of the Synchronicity Code. But even here, the odds of hit are below chance. If we limit our analysis to the TimeMarks at .33, .382, .5, .618, and .66, each of the 5 Marks would be considered a hit one year before and one year after the date of the Mark itself, so each Mark has a "width" of two years. Thus, 5 possible Marks times 2 gives 10

years out of the 78, or a 1 in 8 chance that a hit is a random occurrence. This is a crude measure, but if hits at this level of accuracy occurred across a broad sample size, it would have statistical relevance.

5. *Is the Synchronicity Code only accurate to within a year of a Mark?* No. There are times when the timeline pattern jumps to higher levels of precision, which is one of the strongest proofs that the discovery is a true one. Where the odds of hitting a Mark may be one in ten or two in ten on the yearly scale, the odds might be one in a thousand or less when higher levels of accuracy are achieved. We have and will continue to show a number of these higher level correlations as we proceed. However, even on the yearly scale, you will often see that the hits occur within half a year of the calendar date in which the Mark occurs, which would allow one to reduce the margin for error. This makes the statistical significance of the hit more robust.

One can also take the first and middle date and project a future third date based on the same mathematical ratios. This is a slightly different calculation and is used when you want to project a future third event that is yet to occur. Here's how to do this:

1. Again pick the two dates that you want to study, such as the date when you were born and when an important event happened in your life.

2.   Take the duration between these two dates and multiply it by:
>   (i) 1.5 (one-third),
>   (ii) 1.618 (inverse Fibonacci ratio),
>   (iii) 2.0 (doubled),
>   (iv) 2.618 (the Fibonacci ratio),
>   (v) and 3.0 (tripled)

3.   Add the calculated figures to the date you were born and you will have 5 possible Marks to look for a significant third event, completing the initial triad. Again, other multipliers are possible beyond the 5 shown, such as 1.25 and 1.33.

As an example, if you took my dad's birth year of 1929 and the date he moved into his lifelong home (1959) and added the product of the intervening 30 years multiplied by 1.618, you get 2007, the year of his death. I wouldn't rely on this kind of thing without supporting factors, but one might have looked for a significant event in 2007 on this basis. You should also not expect that all significant events will find precise correlation to an observable timeline. Which events correlate precisely and which don't—that is in itself interesting and may tell us something about the individual that we otherwise would not see. If you find yourself frustrated in your research because you are not finding the hits you are expecting, remember to *follow the coincidences*, for they will rarely lead you astray.

A remarkable case between mother and children

I want to tell you a story that illustrates a variation of the Synchronicity Code pattern, which "rolls backwards." In order to picture it, first imagine there is a huge ruler with 1233 inches marked on it. Then, with the help of your friends, imagine you are going to do an end over end measurement with this ruler, but before you do, you guess, and mark on the ground, where you think the end of the ruler will hit 13,563 inches (1233 x 11) which is over a thousand feet away. How likely is it that your mark on the ground would come within 1 inch of the actual Mark? That's analogous to what the Synchronicity Code achieved with the birthdates of my wife and children.

Here's what happened. In recent years I have made it a point to create something in connection with holiday gift giving for my family. I would write a poem, compose a song, write a little story. This last year I decided to look at the Synchronicity Code to see if there was a link between the kids and my wife's birthdays. Wow was there ever. For their privacy I won't give specific birth dates, but the relative dates are accurate. Our twins were born 1233 days after our oldest son. If you take this interval and "roll it backwards" eleven times, you arrive within 1 day of my wife's birth date. The fact that it is 11 times doesn't matter. It could have been 10, or 12 or 13[9]. What matters is that it rolled over

---

[9] Actually, the fact that it was 11 times *was* significant, as it made the duration between the two outermost dates 40 years. 40 years is an expression of the "Power of Ten" corollary rule, which is discussed in Chapter 5.

to exactly the right spot in the cycle from decades earlier. That is utterly precise. Miraculous even. Now consider that this is *my* family, the guy who came up with the Synchronicity Code. I wasn't picking and choosing among families of relatives and friends to find this match. I set out to find *the very time link* that I found. It was like hitting a hole in one. You may not yet believe. I believe.

Example of Jacqueline Kennedy

Here's how we would "mark time" on a yearly timeframe (in this example we won't worry about the exact count to the day) using the life of Jacqueline Kennedy:

1.   Pick the two measuring dates: here it is Jacqueline's birth in 1929 and her death in 1994.

2.   Take these two outside dates and count the number of years between these dates. Divide this duration into:

> (i) .33 (one-third), which gave 1951
> (ii) .382 (inverse Fibonacci ratio), which gave 1953
> (iii) .5 (half), which gave 1961
> (iv) .618 (Fibonacci ratio), which gave 1968, and
> (v) .66 (two-thirds), which gave 1972.

- **Born** 1929
-
- .33 1951 (?)
-
- **.382** 1953   Marries JFK

42

-
- **.5**: 1961 John F. Kennedy inaugurated. Jackie moves into the White House
-
- **.618** 1968 Marries Onassis
-
- .66 (1972?)
-
- **Dies** 1994

Jacqueline Kennedy on her wedding day

Each of these events occurred at TimeMarks accurate to within a year. Even though accurate only to within one year, it is a statistically valid expression of the Synchronicity Code. Bear in mind that most naturally-occurring cycles are considered valid despite variations in the precise timing of the peaks and valleys of the cycles. Assuming that we pre-determined to use only the five divisions shown above (1/3, .382, 1/2, .618, 2/3), since Jackie only lived 65 years, any one significant hit would have a 10 (5 Marks, 2 years width) in 65 chance, or 1.5 in 10 of occurring just by chance. 2 hits would by 10/65 X 10/65 = .023, or around 2 chances in a 100. Here we have 3 hits, so the chances are 10/65 X 10/65 X 10/65 = .0036, or about four chances in a thousand that this is pure coincidence.

"Ok, but you've mixed marriages and the inauguration/move into the White House. That's picking and choosing."

I accept that. To make the probability calculation more robust, and again this is just for illustration purposes, let's just focus on the marriage dates. (This is the basis of a sample study we undertake with the founding father Presidents and their wives later on.) Now the probability would be based on the 2 mirror hits at .382 and .618: 10/65 x 10/65 = .02366, or a little over 2 chances in a hundred that the correlation was just a random happening. Could it be pure chance? Absolutely. Was it? After seeing many much more precise correlations than this, I don't think so.

Let me reiterate that this is not about natural cycles like the tides, biorhythms, changes in the seasons, or other known, regularly recurring cycles. The Synchronicity Code is something different. Events that have no apparent causal relationship are linked together,

44

by *the time interval* itself. There is no known cause. One can theorize that the numeric divisions of time act as a field, like ripples when a stone is thrown in a pond, only the ripples move across time, and thus appear to cause the future event.

At this point I still haven't presented you with some of the most striking evidence. As we proceed, if at some point you get the eerie feeling that maybe, just maybe, we're "not in Kansas anymore", then you and I will be on the same page.

3

HOW
I
DISCOVERED
THE SYNCHRONICITY CODE

Every ultimate fact is only the first in a new series. Ralph
    Waldo Emerson

    I am a lawyer by profession. While I strive for a
high degree of competence, the law has never been a
labor of love for me. Even when I was a law student, my
philosophical soul had wanderlust. One day I wandered
over to the business school library and found myself
captivated by the literature on a peculiar type of

"technical analysis" of the markets.   This might not seem so "philosophical", but one thing had caught my eye.   Future's Magazine was running ads by Robert Fischer for his "Golden Section Compass" trading methodology.   This trading method introduced me to Fibonacci ratios as they are applied to the markets, and which (now) have been applied to history via the Synchronicity Code.   To me, this represented a hidden, universal order that lay behind, and transcended the mundane aspects of Wall Street.   While I have generally traded successfully, I have wisely never relied solely on investing to make my living.   But ever since then I have been an avid student of the markets and have held my own as an active investor, based solely on mathematical and geometric relationships between turning points in the markets.

I made the Synchronicity Code discovery because my years of researching and trading the markets trained me to see mathematical patterns that others might not see.

One day early in 2009, while having a casual conversation with an office colleague, I said (as if I knew what I was talking about) that the mathematical analysis I used in trading the markets must apply to everything, "down to your very sneezes".   Of the two of us, I think I was more struck by this statement than he was.   Soon I was feverishly researching people, dates and events. From the start I found one after another of striking time correlations between events, all stemming from the simple idea that three or more meaningfully-related events could be mathematically linked across time.

Meaningful correlations happened so often that I quickly became convinced that I was on to something.

What surprises me is that I hadn't thought of this before. After years of seeing turning points form in the markets at precise intervals, I should have clued in that markets are just made up of actions by ordinary people— millions of them, to be sure—but those actions are just like any other action on the stage of life. The main reason that this truth is discernable in the markets is that the numerical aspects of the chart are right there in front of your eyes, consisting of the time (x axis) and price (y axis) of the stock (or commodity or forex pair, or whatever). *The markets are life plotted on a graph.* Of course, I reasoned, if these patterns exist in the markets, they had to be in everything, because stock charts are just mathematical snapshots of unfolding events. I began to wonder whether *all* events organize themselves according to the duration of time between events.[10]

Those few readers who have studied market-timing theories may interject, and rightly so, that the old

---

[10] I reiterate that you will not be able to find a Synchronicity Code correlation for every event that happens. However, if *any* events are arranged in accordance with the timeline pattern, then the events that precede or follow such aligned events must presumably also be so arranged, otherwise the overall pattern could not manifest. A way to think about this is to picture 3 mountain peaks arranged so that the distance between the first two peaks is mathematically related to the third peak. Let's say that peaks 1 and 2 are 1000 yards apart and the third peak, along a single line of sight, is 500 yards beyond that—so that peak 2 is 2/3^{rds} of the distance between peaks 1 and 3. In order for this arrangement to form, all the rivers, valleys, trees and slopes that comprise the mountain range are instrumental to the overall mathematical relationship. So it is with events across time.

master timers R. N. Elliott or W. D. Gann also taught that events beyond the markets are mathematically and cyclically linked. It is even said that Gann predicted the surprise attack by the Japanese at Pearl Harbor and the outcome of World War II using yearly cycles based on a version of the Power of Ten, which is discussed in the following chapter. Quite right. I give credit to these pioneers for their discoveries in this area. But neither R.N. Elliott, W.D. Gann, nor any other researcher to my knowledge, has heretofore theorized the link between meaningful coincidences and time cycles.

For me, finding the expressions of the Synchronicity Code in historical events has been a revelation, in part because these concepts were in the back of my mind for decades before I started exploring their ramifications outside of the markets. I understand why it took so long for me to see this. While my market studies took notice of purely linear time relationships, like a Synchronicity Code pattern, my own trading research focused on the x- and y- axes in one circular motion.[11]

Let me explain what I mean. The markets have a time dimension and a price dimension. At the time I was introduced to Fibonacci ratios, little research outside of the work of W.D. Gann was being conducted to integrate these dimensions. Over time, my own work began to bring in the vertical price element to the time dimension, using *the geometry of the circle*. Thus it was that I grew

---

[11] An example of a circular pattern governing the 1929 crash is shown in Chapter 10.

to consider the time element alone as only a part of the picture and not the whole. Since events outside the markets have time but there was no obvious counterpart of a vertical or circular dimension (as there was no chart to embody this), I steered away from considering them. Once I overcame this hesitancy, I quickly discovered that purely "horizontal" time calculations can indeed correlate external events, and research into the Synchronicity Code took off on its own.

Nevertheless, one must still wonder if there is a "vertical" or "circular" dimension to the Synchronicity Code out there in the world of non-market events that has yet to be uncovered. This issue may one day have to be faced in order to fully understand the Synchronicity Code's expressions of historical (and personal) events across time. But that is not for today.

Parenthetically, I have long since concluded that the markets are indeed regulated by a hidden, geometric or mathematical order. This does not necessarily mean that one can easily forecast things in advance, for the primary reason that order can express itself in more than one way. Think of it this way. The stock market forms an important bottom in March of 2009. Let's imagine for a moment that the end of the ensuing trend will occur on the radius of some circle, the perimeter of which could be predicted in advance, but which like electrons around a nucleus, "radiates" at different levels, so in fact there are several concentric circles expanding on the basis of fractions or multiples of the base circle. If the market indeed stops at a forecast perimeter, one would be right that this was an expression of inherent geometric order.

But there is a catch. The market could turn for a bit, then shoot up to the next larger perimeter before the trend really ends. By stopping at any predicted perimeter, the expression of underlying order is there. But to successfully predict a turning point, and profit from such prediction, you also need to know which vibration level governs. And then you need to know when to get out at the end of the ensuing trend. It may be possible, but it is "no cheap thing".[12]

"How come no one discovered the Synchronicity Code before you?"

I have already noted Gann's contributions. So I am not the first to claim that there are time cycles in history. What is new is the link to synchronicity. Now I naturally tend to think outside the box. Plus I have a strong interest in philosophy and psychology. I have also intensely researched cycles in the markets, a true labor of love for me. But perhaps it is the relatively recent advent of the internet that enabled the extensive research into the timing of historical events to be conducted at the touch of a button. Very few others would have this combination of circumstances before them.

---

[12] In Chapter 10, I give some examples of how mathematical analysis of time and price can be applied to forecast market trends. I should emphasize that many skeptics believe that such patterns in the markets do not exist. I strongly disagree. This being said, seeing mathematical relationships in hindsight is one thing, predicting them in real time and profiting from them is altogether more challenging. We address prediction using the Synchronicity Code in Chapter 12.

In the next chapter, we reflect on C.G. Jung's theory of synchronicity. The Synchronicity Code expands the reach of Jung's theory, because *it brings map-like order to experiences of synchronicity as they unfold across time.* No longer is synchronicity the "just-so" story of two meaningfully related events occurring at one time. Now one must look at every experience of synchronicity and wonder if it is part of an unfolding series, across time, placing its Mark on an unknown future.

Mandala made by a patient of Jung

4

C.G. JUNG AND SYNCHRONICITY

Who has fully realized that history is not contained in thick books but lives in our very blood? C.G. Jung

The occurrence of synchronicity, Carl Jung's term for "meaningful coincidence" is one of the surest guides for when the Synchronicity Code is at work. When you see a pair of events separated by the passage of time exhibiting a strong coincidence or coincidences, be on the look out for a third meaningful event (or more) that follows (or preceded it) in sequence.

Merriam-Webster awkwardly defines the term "synchronicity" as "the coincidental occurrence of events and especially psychic events (as similar thoughts in widely separated persons or a mental image of an unexpected event before it happens) that seem related but are not explained by conventional mechanisms of causality—used especially in the psychology of C. G. Jung." But for our purposes it is just as well to say "meaningful coincidences" and leave it at that. The theory was first raised by Jung in the 1920s, but lectured upon and written about much later in his career, in the 1951 Eranos lecture, and published in an essay, *Synchronicity—An Acausal Connecting Principle*, in 1952.

Jung's ideas on synchronicity most likely stemmed from his study of Chinese Taoist philosophy, in particular the I Ching, or Book of Changes. The most frequently recounted incident took place during one of Jung's psychotherapy sessions. A woman patient recited a dream involving a piece of jewelry in the form of a golden scarab (a type of beetle). As she was talking, Jung heard a tapping from the outside of the window. He opened the window and in flew a scarabaeid beetle. Jung caught the beetle in his hand and showed it to the patient saying "here is your scarab". The incident was reported as a turning point in the patient's treatment.

In the scarab story, an inner event—the woman's dream—came together with an outer event—the scarab beetle at the window, which occurred at the moment in time when the woman was recounting her dream. This was a meaningful coincidence, which upon seeing it, served to loosen up the mindset of the patient. The event was particularly striking to Jung for to him golden scarabs were archetypally significant, dating back to the ancient Egyptians, for whom the scarab was a symbol of rebirth.

In addition to drawing from Eastern philosophical and spiritual traditions, Jung's ideas on synchronicity appear to have been influenced by Austrian biologist Paul Kammerer, who researched and catalogued coincidences, formulating a theory of "seriality". In *Das Gesetz der Serie* (The Law of the Series), written in 1919, Kammerer postulated that all events are connected by unknown forces (conceived of as waves of seriality) which resulted in a periodic clustering of coincidences. Kammerer would, for example, observe passersby in public parks and record what he saw as a clustering of those who carried umbrellas. While the objective science behind Kammerer's theory has been criticized, his work appears to be the first attempt to observe coincidences from a scientific perspective. Einstein was of the opinion that Kammerer's theory was "interesting, and by no means absurd".

One thing I like about Kammerer's theory is that seriality does not challenge the notion of causality. Rather, it postulates that events may be grouped by cause and also that they may be grouped by *meaning*. This requires a mind to perceive the meaning. It brings to mind the scientifically verified principle in quantum physics that, at least at the quantum level, the observer affects the observed. In fact, Jung extensively collaborated with distinguished physicist Wolfgang Pauli during the years when Jung was formulating the synchronicity principle. Pauli may have encouraged Jung to emphasize the significance of meaning in the integration of acausal, synchronous phenomenon with causal events in the physical world.[13] But it is also just what we find in the Synchronicity Code—that events across time are linked mathematically because they contain some kind of shared meaning.

This isn't what I believed when I first starting researching the Synchronicity Code. I thought that virtually any two conceptually-related events—down to your sneezes—would be linked across time. Now I would say that it takes the human perception of meaning to link three or more events across time, according to the natural time divisions of the Synchronicity Code.

I used to pooh-pooh it when I heard the new age axiom that "there are no accidents or coincidences, everything is synchronicity." But with the advent of the Synchronicity Code, I no longer feel it is so far off the mark. The Synchronicity Code evidences a heretofore unknown, yet *primary driver* of the events of human history. We are no longer on an analyst's couch recounting a dream when something taps on the window. We are at the heart of war, politics, religion, invention

---

[13] Pauli was known among his peers for apparently causing a mysterious failure in technical equipment by his very presence, something which they labeled "the Pauli Effect".

and each other event that moves us deeply. It is profound and far-reaching.

Kammerer's work required that he count coincidences occurring over time. The Synchronicity Code, in contrast, counts the interval of time between events. Neither quite fits the traditional notion of synchronicity, with its focus on a single moment in time when the meaningful coincidence occurs. That "moment" can be stretched a bit to a few hours or a day, but that's about it. However, if Jung's theory is to serve as a framework for the Synchronicity Code, the theory of synchronicity must be expanded to encompass multiple timeframes.

Here's why it makes sense to do so. First, not all meaningful coincidences occur simultaneously. For example, the well-known multiple coincidences between the circumstances surrounding Abraham Lincoln and John F. Kennedy and their assassinations could well be seen as "meaningful", yet they are separated by nearly a century.

As another example, this time over a much shorter time period, recently I had a "traditional" experience of synchronicity while I was researching possible Synchronicity Code sequences related to earthquakes (in light of Japan's Sendai Tsunami) and read about "coronal mass ejections" from the sun as possibly linked to earthquakes. Later that evening I watched a program on television which again theorized that coronal mass ejections could possibly trigger dangerous weather events on Earth. To my recollection, this was the first time that I had ever heard this term, and it struck me as a "meaningful coincidence". Yet the two experiences occurred several hours apart, not simultaneously.

If simultaneity were the sine qua non of synchronicity, these experiences would have to be excluded. It would require that we come up with an entirely new concept for these types of meaningful coincidences if the Jungian notion of synchronicity does not cover them.

Second, the *meaning* in meaningful coincidences often makes reference to other points in time. A few years ago, my wife and I were considering moving to a larger house and arranged to look at an antique home called "Bluebird Farm" located one town over. As I was leaving my office to meet my wife and the broker at the property, a beautiful, bright blue bird landed a few feet from me and flitted about for a few moments before flying away. I immediately felt this was an experience of synchronicity, and was somewhat puzzled later on that the house did not turn out to be what we were looking for. It was only recently—a few years later—that the possible meaning of the synchronicity became clear.

As I child, I spent my summers on a 100-acre farm owned by my grandparents, which was next door to my cousins, in East Longmeadow, Massachusetts. Across the street, my uncle operated a large farm stand called "Bluebird Acres". I have fond memories of spending the afternoons playing with my cousins out in the apple orchards. On one occasion when I was a little older, I had what I would call a "luminous" experience of *the land* while walking in one of the orchards. Perhaps more than any other, this experience defined for me what makes a physical place, along with one's family, a "true home". The meaning of the synchronous experience, it now seems, was that "you will know when you find your true place to call home". From one perspective, the synchronicity was about the moment when I noticed the blue bird on my way to see Bluebird Farm. But the meaning traversed time, from my childhood days, to house hunting, to the point years later when I realized that the synchronicity was about something larger than the afternoon's house hunting.

Taking again the Lincoln-Kennedy assassinations, the series of meaningful coincidences became fully apparent only after Kennedy's death. That could be thought of as the one moment where history and event achieved some sort of simultaneity. But the meaning was found in its relation to events that occurred a century earlier.

Third, the observable synchronicity can consist of *time itself*. How odd that two cousins were born on the same day three years apart and they are such fast friends! How strange that Grandma died on the 50th anniversary of the day of her wedding to Grandpa and she always said her wedding was the favorite day of her life.

Of course, the Synchronicity Code, by definition, is all about traversing time. In some senses it is closer to Kammerer's seriality than Jung's concept. But it differs from seriality in both the selection of what coincidences are considered meaningful (clustering of passersby with umbrellas would count for Kammerer but wouldn't count here) and in terms of the use of precise time periods to pinpoint events in a series.

Like Kammerer's work, the Synchronicity Code could move Jung's theory of synchronicity toward a quantifiable footing. With time comes the possibility of counting. With counting comes the possibility of scientific, statistical analysis. In any case, the Synchronicity Code can otherwise serve to validate a synchronous experience, since the *added* coincidence of a precise time correlation makes the initial set of coincidences that much more unlikely to be pure chance.

As a final thought, I have wondered about the woman analysand in Jung's beetle story. The question is whether *every* experience of synchronicity is in fact a Mark on a Synchronicity Code timeline. Was her dream and breakthrough part of a larger pattern over time? We many never know. But it is something to track in one's own life. The next time you experience synchronicity, note the time!

5

THE POWER OF TEN

But I was thinking of a way to multiply by ten, and always, in the answer, get the question back again.
Lewis Carroll

There are three main principles (so far) in applying the Synchronicity Code. The first is the theory itself, which postulates that an event will occur at fractions or multiples of the duration between two other meaningfully related events. The second is to "follow the coincidences," based on the fact that a Code pattern can most reliably be observed in cases where a coincidence is evidenced in the two base measuring dates.

The third is the Power of Ten.

Recall the Napoleon-Charlemagne timeline from Chapter 1 in which major events in the lives of French conquerors were linked by a timeline spanning 1000 years. We now introduce a further corollary rule to the Synchronicity Code: that significant events often synchronously occur according to the multiples of ten: 10 years (20 years, 30 years, etc.), 100 years, 1000 years, and so on. The half and quarter marks of these multiples can also be important as sub-cycle indications that the Power of Ten is at work. Perhaps this rule has something to do with the fact that our Gregorian calendar and decimal system is based on the power of ten, so if events are meaningfully arranged in the calendar system that means the most to us, the Power of Ten is an implicit root building block.

I am not the first to discover the role of the Power of Ten in the cycles of history, nor am I sure of the original source, which I suspect is lost to antiquity. As mentioned in Chapter 3, the early 20th century stock forecaster W.D. Gann taught that all things (not just the stock market) run in cycles, of which 1000 year and 100 year cycles were paramount. These cycles were then subdivided into subcycles, of which the 50 year, 20 year and 10 year cycles were considered to be of importance. In order to forecast a future event, one would go back to the circumstances that existed 10, 20, 50 years ago and look for parallels.

I don't find this *always* to be true. For example, nothing comparable to the signing of the Declaration of Independence happened in 1876. Nothing comparable to the first powered flight of the Wright Brothers occurred in 2003 (100 years after the first flight at Kitty Hawk). And yet there often *does* seem to be something to this, when aligned with the Synchronicity Code. Here are some examples:

1. Abraham Lincoln was assassinated in 1865; JFK was assassinated nearly a 100 years later, in 1963 (-2).
2. The stock market peaked on October 8, 2007, followed by a market crash related to the subprime mortgage crisis. Almost exactly 100 years earlier, in mid-October of 1907, the Panic of 1907 was triggered by a failed attempt to corner the copper market.
3. Hammurabi commenced his rule in 1795 BC and wrote the Code of Hammurabi. Napoleon took control of France in 1799 and issued his Napoleonic Code in 1804, which considering the vast time span, is close to the Mark over 3600 years later. (The two zeros at the end of 3600 make this a Power of Ten correlation.) We already encountered this phenomenon in the Buddha, Christ, Mohammed timeline; when the BC and AD dates straddle the "zero" date (at the time of Christ), which is itself an expression of the Power of Ten.

4. Lincoln issued the Emancipation Proclamation in 1863. The Civil Rights Act was signed by President Lyndon Johnson in 1964.

5. The death of JFK, Jr. in 1999 was at the confluence of a near exact 70 (10 x 7) year period from his mother's birth, and a 30 (10 x 3) year period from his uncle's Chappaquiddick incident.

6. The Pearl Harbor attack occurred in December 1941. Sixty years later (10 x 6), on September 11, 2001, the second great "surprise attack" occurred with the attacks at the World Trade Center and Pentagon. As we have already seen, an accurate Code timeline links 9/11 back to Pearl Harbor. The Power of Ten may have been a key factor behind the tremendous magnitude of the event.

7. On September 3, 1929, the stock market peaked, leading to the Great Depression. Strangely, almost exactly ten years later, on September 1, 1939, Nazi Germany invaded Poland, igniting WWII. As doubly strange as this may seem, just shy of ten years further, on August 29, 1949, the USSR fired its first nuclear test weapon, which might aptly be considered the initiation of the Cold War. While these events are not neatly categorized as to their meaning, they do spell impending doom and express the Power of Ten. I thus call this the *Omigod Cycle*, and discuss it again in Chapter 12 dealing with predicting the future.

I would not use the Power of Ten as a stand alone tool for navigating future events. Its power lies in "triangulating" it with a Synchronicity Code timeline. For example, in Chapter 9, I will show you the timeline that warned me that the stock market might make an important top in October of 2007. This correlation was made more reliable, and the turning point of greater magnitude, because it dovetailed (triangulated) with the historic fact that a significant market panic began 100 years earlier, in October of 1907.

A Strange Case of Inventors and Composers

The following Power of Ten case is one that I probably would *not* count as evidence of the Synchronicity Code because it mixes and matches in a peculiar way, but it is intriguing nonetheless. The base coincidence is the birth of Wolfgang Amadeus Mozart on January 27, 1756 followed by the birth of Spanish composer Juan Arriaga on January 27, 1806, exactly 50 years later to the day. Arriaga was not well known outside of Spain, but there are a number of parallels between the two men that add teeth to the calendar date coincidence. Both men were gifted child prodigies and died young. Both left their native countries and found success in Paris. There were similarities in their musical styles. Their birth names were closely related: Mozart's was Johannes Chrysostomus and Arriaga's was Juan Crisotomo. Finally, after his death, Arriaga was nicknamed the "Spanish Mozart".

Clearly this is a pairing that would qualify for a closer look via the Synchronicity Code. Additionally, the 50 year span invites Power of Ten analysis to see what occurs at the 100-year Mark. One should look both before and after the dates of the base pair. When we do so, we find connections in both directions, but the nature of creative ingenuity modulates from music composition to the field of invention.

Benjamin Franklin was born on January 17, 1706, within less than two weeks from the exact birth of Mozart 50 years later. Leaving aside for the moment that Franklin had little to do with composing music, the timeline is clear:

- **Franklin** born January 17, 1706
-
-
-
-
- 1/2 Mark: **Mozart** born January 27, 1756
-
-
-
-
-
- **Arriaga** born January 27, 1806

Is this a valid expression of the Synchronicity Code? I am in doubt. Franklin was a skilled and knowledgeable musician, but he was not known as a composer. He invented a beautiful musical instrument called the glass armonica, which figures prominently in the "Dance of the Sugar Plum Fairy" in Tchaikowsky's Nutcracker Ballet. Mozart himself composed several pieces for the instrument. But in his day Franklin was famous not for music, nor even for politics. He was famous the world over *as an inventor*. During the Revolutionary War, as ambassador to France, Franklin's fame preceded him as the inventor of the lightening rod. His other inventions included the Franklin stove, bifocals and the odometer.

What makes this case so interesting is that if we look for a Power of Ten Mark 100 years *after* Mozart, we get a hit, but again we don't get a composer. We get an inventor! Nicola Tesla was born July 10, 1856, which is about six months from the exact Mark over a 150 year span. While Tesla never achieved the fame or fortune of Thomas Edison, Tesla was Edison's equal (or better) in his inventive genius.

The intriguing thing about this is that we all know of Franklin's famous, albeit dangerous, experiment of flying a kite in a lightening storm to attract electricity down the kite wire to a metal key. Yet Tesla too was focused on electricity, where he developed alternating current, the AC motor, the polyphase system of electrical distribution, and patented inventions related to the collection of electricity from the atmosphere. One could not think of a better forbear in history for Tesla than Benjamin Franklin.

It is also interesting that the compositions or inventions, as the case may be, came to both Mozart and Tesla in completely-realized form. Mozart would see the entire score in his mind and then simply went through the exercise of writing it down. Similarly, Tesla's inventions came to him ready-made in highly detailed visual imagery.

I'm not sure what to make of this mixing and matching of composers and inventors. The dates seem to tie together well and the composer to composer and inventor to inventor parallels are strong. I am tempted to lump the four of them into the category of "creative geniuses", but think it is better to simply note the pattern for future reference, should something similar arise again.

* * *

There are other number systems other than the Power of Ten that may have significance to the unfolding patterns of the Synchronicity Code. In particular, patterns derived from the number 7, also known as the "Law of Octaves," are the subject of ongoing research by the author.

"I cannot tell a lie"

6

LIES,
DAMN LIES,
AND
THE FOUNDING FATHER
PRESENTS

Not everything that can be counted counts, and not everything that counts can be counted. Albert Einstein

How do we go about proving that the Synchronicity Code is a real phenomenon? If we want to put this theory to the test, we have to postulate a result and then obtain the predicted outcome over many tries. Why do we need to do this? Because the scientific method is built on the *law of large numbers*. A theory can't be proven until you obtain the predicted outcome over many tests.

The law of large numbers by the way is actually an admission by science that uncertainty often prevails in making single predictions of single events.[14] Indeed, the work of Bohr and Heisenberg in quantum physics has elevated chance to an objective aspect of nature. Jung's brilliant student, Marie-Louise von Franz, would question, when analyzing synchronous events, whether we should apply probability analysis at all. For von Franz, the "proof" lies in the numinous feeling-response to an experience of synchronicity.

For the Synchronicity Code, the answer may lie in both the realms of science and feeling.

To determine whether an occurrence is not just chance, one would apply the following criteria:

1. *The ordered pattern must serve some purpose or function.* In this case we hypothesize that the Synchronicity Code pattern is integral to how events unfold, that they are related to a root cause (but not necessarily the only cause) of the timing of the events. The function of the ordered pattern is to bring about the effect of events themselves.

2. *The ordered pattern must be specific and complex.* By "specific", we mean that the pattern must tie to events at specified points. For our

---

[14] As observed by Marie-Louise von Franz in On Divination and Synchronicity, The Psychology of Meaningful Chance, Studies in Jungian Psychology by Jungian Analysts, 1980, Lecture 1.

purposes, this is implicit in the unique calendar dates of events themselves. "Complexity" deals with order that is non-repetitious. If the dog presses down the "s" key on your computer keyboard, he will produce an ordered sequence of "d's" across the screen. But this order lacks the complexity of typing, say, this sentence. Archduke Ferdinand's getting in an open car to sit beside his wife in Sarajevo is clearly a specific and complex patterning of time and events culminating in his assassination at a precise point in time.[15]

3.   *There must be no known law of nature that, by itself, could have caused the ordered pattern.* While there are cyclic rhythms in nature, such as the 11-year sunspot cycle, there is no known law of nature that causes the linking of historical events across time by the numeric divisions of the Synchronicity Code.

4.   *There must be no random process of chance which explains the apparent ordering.* Now granted, this is the thing we are trying to find out. The test may well be the sheer unlikelihood of, say, an occurrence happening by chance that has odds of 1 in 10,000. Even then, "proof" requires a much higher statistical measure. The French mathematician Emile Borel came up with what he considered a standard by which a statistical probability of something happening by pure chance to be zero: 1 in 10^{50}. This is 10 to the 50th

---

[15] We will show how this event unfolds on a Synchronicity Code timeline in Chapter 8.

power, the equivalent of having 50 zeros. The level of statistical evidence presented here is no where near Borel's Law. That's why the best we can offer is *evidence* and not *proof.*

Bear in mind that each time I show you yet another Synchronicity Code example and you consider whether it is a random pattern or not, the stakes are raised. They can't *all* be random coincidences, could they? If an apparent hit occurs in one individual's life, it's interesting, just like tossing only 1 head in 10 is (mildly) interesting, expecting, as you would, around 5 heads. But when you do this ten times in a row, and then do *that* ten times in a row, just maybe it is evidence that what is going on is not due to chance.

A common, and correct, criticism by statisticians is that what seems to be an extraordinary coincidence is something that has to happen anyway. Someone *is* going to win the lottery, although it is a 1 in 200 Million chance that it will be anyone in particular. In poker, we just do not notice when we get a hand that consists of a pair of twos and a jack. But this hand is just as unique, in its specific configuration, as getting a royal flush. What distinguishes the Synchronicity Code is: (i) in each case we are looking at a *pre-selected, specified, small group* for meaningfully-related events on dates aligned to whole number time divisions, (ii) in some instances the search is narrowed to a single possible Mark, as when two different, but related Synchronicity Code sequences are triangulated, and (iii) finally, the Synchronicity Code is not just used to find correlations in the past; it is also used to predict specific outcomes in the future, making the chance of it being a random occurrence much more unlikely.

A pre-selected, specified, small group

Investigating the Synchronicity Code using statistics has its unique challenges, in part because the necessity of finding *patterns of meaning* limits application to a broad data set. But it may be possible. We can get at this issue in the following way. To start, we need to find a test group that is objective and also easily verifiable. At first I considered looking at the Founding Fathers. There certainly were some interesting tidbits to work with. Patrick Henry gave his signature speech "give me liberty or give me death" at his .618 Mark. Paul Revere took his famous ride at his 50% Mark. Alexander Hamilton was shot to death by Aaron Burr in a duel on the .618 Mark of Burr's life[16]. There is uncertainty in this selection, however. Should we include John Hancock and Samuel Adams and leave out, say, Patrick Henry and John Jay? Historians may debate who belongs on the final list of the so-called "Founding Fathers".

Where there can be no debate is the list of those Founding Fathers who also served as American

---

[16] Of course, the death of Hamilton cannot also appear as a Mark in his own life, as his death constitutes a final outside date from which the other Marks are calculated. It is inherently the case also, that seminal events in a person's life that occur near to an individual's date of death will not be recorded near one of the primary internal Marks. But in those cases, one should continue to look for "rolling cycles" like the one found between the two World Trade Center attacks and Pearl Harbor, using the late-in-life event and the death date as the two base measuring dates.

Presidents: Washington, Adams, Jefferson, Madison and Monroe. Their history is well documented so it is easy to create accurate Synchronicity Code timelines of their lives.

Corollary rule number one says "follow the coincidences". With the Founding Father presidents, there is one particular coincidence that is second only to the Lincoln-Kennedy series of coincidences when it comes to American Presidents. This is the fact that Thomas Jefferson and John Adams *died on the same day*. But it wasn't just any day. That day was *fifty years from the signing of the Declaration of Independence*. But it wasn't just in the fiftieth year; these two Founding Father Presidents died *exactly* 50 years later, on July 4, 1826.

Pretty stunning. I think the reason it occurred at all is because meaningful coincidences are part and parcel of how events unfold across time pursuant to the Synchronicity Code.

Here is how the Synchronicity Code choreographed events over this 50 year time span. Jefferson was inaugurated on March 4, 1801. Given that the inauguration date was mandated, there could not be a more exact midpoint between the signing of the Declaration of Independence and Jefferson's death for the inauguration to occur than this date.[17] The kicker is that at this precise moment, the baton was passed to Jefferson from the out-going president, *none other than John*

---

[17] July 4, 1801 would of course be the exact date, but the Presidential inauguration was (until the 20th Constitutional Amendment in 1933) held on March 4th in the year following the election.

Adams. One can imagine the two men shaking hands, a bolt of lightening marking the skies at that moment. In fact, Adams had left Washington before the inauguration, making him one of only 4 surviving presidents who did not attend his own successor's inauguration. While Adams and Jefferson were not close at the time (they grew closer in their old age), Adams' absence was likely due to the despondent mood of Adams following the death of his alcoholic son Charles a few months earlier. We will revisit Adams melancholy with respect to another President's timeline below.

Jefferson and Adams

- **Declaration of Independence** signed July 4, 1776
-
-
- 1/2 Mark: March 4, 1801 **Jefferson inaugurated, Adams presidency ends**
-
-
- **Both Jefferson and Adams die on the same day** July 4, 1826

Now our present objective is to see if a statistical study of the Synchronicity Code could be developed using Founding Father American Presidents as a study set. We began with the startling coincidence that both Jefferson and Adams died on July 4th exactly 50 years following the signing of the Declaration of Independence. But this only involves the two men. We can expand the study by again following the coincidence, this time adding to our data set any President that was born or died on July 4th of any year. This adds two names to our list: James Monroe, a Founding Father who died July 4, 1831, and Calvin Coolidge, who was born July 4, 1872. Calvin Coolidge obviously wasn't a Founding Father, and his connection is a birth date, not a death date, but let's include him anyway. The data set is still pretty exclusive, you have to have been a president that was born or died on July 4th.

James Monroe (April 28, 1758 – July 4, 1831) was only the fifth President of the United States, and the third to die on the 4th of July. 3 out of the first 5! That alone qualifies as a Synchronicity Code sequence: you could roll the 5 year span between the Jefferson/Adams and Monroe deaths back ten times to hit 1776. Further, the timing of Monroe's death in 1831 not only marked the 4th of July but also aligned with the signing of the Declaration of Independence on the 25% Mark of his life (1831-1758 = 73 x .25 = 18.25. 1758 + 18.25 = 1776+). The exact Mark was August 13th, less than 6 weeks from the 4th of July. (Here we would have to think that the precision of the Mark gave way to perfect precision of the July 4th anniversary date.) The duration from 1776 to his death also aligns with the .75 Mark in 1817, the year President Monroe was inaugurated (exact Mark: October 3).

James Monroe (5th President)

- **Born** April 28, 1758
-
- 1/4 Mark: **4th of July 1776** (*Exact mark: August 13, 1776—less than 6 weeks from exact date*)
-
-
-
- **Dies** July 4, 1831 *Exactly 5 years after Jefferson and Adams and 55 years after the signing of the Declaration*

Monroe Timeline commencing July 4, 1776

- **4th of July 1776**
-
-
-
- 3/4 Mark: 1817 **Inauguration** (March 4)
-
- **Dies** July 4, 1831

Calvin Coolidge was the thirtieth President of the United States. He presided over the boom times of the roaring Twenties, during which he famously uttered "the [chief] business of American people is business." Here too, there is a timeline link between 1776 and Coolidge's life: Coolidge's birthday falls within 3 and a ½ months of the .382 Mark between 1776 and the date of his death in 1933.

Calvin Coolidge (30th President)

- **4th of July 1776**
-
- .382 **Born** July 4, 1872 (*Exact between two outside dates would be March 24*)
-
-
-
-
-
- **Dies** January 5, 1933

While acknowledging this timeline, I am somewhat at a loss as to why *this* president should join the group of Founding Fathers in the connection with the *meaning* of July 4th, so maybe this one is just plain old chance. Coolidge was born within four years of the First Centennial; but so what. His leadership style was consistent with the laissez-faire principles espoused by Jefferson, but this doesn't impress me either. A stronger link might be found in the emotional side of things. During his re-election campaign, Coolidge's younger son Calvin died of an infection from a blister which formed while he was playing tennis on White House courts. This loss saddened Coolidge greatly, leading him to remark, "When he died, the power and the glory of the presidency went with him." Coolidge was thereafter a stiff, awkward President and man of few words. In these ways he was perhaps not unlike Adams who was not known for his social grace as president. In fact, both Adams and Jefferson also were saddened by the loss of a child's life during their tenure as president. Coolidge also happens to be a distant relative of Adams, as well as to FDR, Gerald Ford and Richard Nixon.

I will leave it to future research to shed light on the meaning, if it is to be found, of Coolidge's link to Adams, Jefferson and Monroe. But if the statistical test is to find a Synchronicity Code Mark based on the coincidental date of Coolidge's birth, then (based on the 1/4 Mark shown above) this case qualifies as a yes.

For now, let's just take Adams, Jefferson and Monroe. Here we have three Presidents, all of whom are considered Founding Fathers. All three exhibit links according to the Synchronicity Code to July 4, 1776, as do the calendar dates of their death. This is to some degree a proof of concept that by beginning with meaningful coincidences (in this case death dates), timeline relationships follow.

It is difficult to assign a probability statistic to these events because the sample size is too small. This illustrates what is likely a recurrent issue, which is that the best and clearest cases of the Synchronicity Code depend on meaningful coincidences and these don't tend to occur en masse. I think the only answer to this is to treat, as our test group, *every case* drawn from major historical events where strong coincidences are found. In this book lies example after example. The amalgamation of all these coincidental timelines constitutes the beginning of a valid statistical sample. To be clear, what

I am saying is that, by beginning with two events that show some meaningful coincidence, that pair of events enters the statistical pool. It enters *before* we apply the Synchronicity Code calculation, so either the Code flies thereafter or it doesn't. This would constitute a valid basis for further statistical analysis.

* * *

Recall my story about how I first stumbled upon the Synchronicity Code following my remark to a colleague that the time cycles I was seeing in the stock market were undoubtedly true about everything, "down to your very sneezes". I am no longer sure of this. Sneezes don't matter. The significance of meaning, to the individual, to a given culture or civilization, appears to be of central importance to the inner workings of the Synchronicity Code.

So we have to keep our sights on meaning. George Washington was our nation's very first president, yet his term of office did not occur on a significant timeline Mark within his own life. Why not? For a man who had one of the most interesting, event-laden lives that one could imagine, the commencement of his term of office may not have been the central thing *in his own eyes*.

What if, *to him,* George Washington were leader of soldiers first, leader of nation second? It is here that we see how the Synchronicity Code metes out the pattern of a man's life. The mantle of "Commander-in-Chief" was placed on Washington's shoulders for the *second* time at the Second Continental Congress in June 1775.

The first time it happened was in 1755, when Lieutenant Governor Robert Dinwiddie of colonial Virginia granted him his commission as commander in chief "in defense of His Majesty's Colony".

The Jumonville Affair

One "coincidence" that seems to have been under-reported in the history books is that George Washington was a pivotal military figure at the start of *both* the Revolutionary War and the French and Indian War, and his actual first combat in both instances went badly. In the first case, Washington was in charge of a company of Virginia militia that ambushed a small force of French Canadiens under the command of Joseph Coulon de Villiers de Jumonville. Jumonville and his men surrendered, but he was then killed while in Washington's custody. The manner in which this happened is the subject of debate among historians. Washington, however, was thereafter captured himself at Fort Necessity in Pennsylvania. He was soon released by his captors, but he was required to sign a statement written in French (which Washington could not read) that admitted that Jumonville was assassinated. This event had international repercussions, which played a material role in the commencement of the Seven Years War (in the American theater this war was known as the French and Indian War.)

The Battle of Long Island

Twenty-two years later, in the first Revolutionary War battle in which shots were fired under Washington's command, and which was in fact the largest battle of the Revolutionary War, things went even worse. Washington made a huge tactical error in leaving one of his flanks wide open. Local loyalists had warned the British that the Jamaica Pass was virtually unprotected. The British under General Clinton led a night march of 10,000 soldiers that split Washington's forces and saw his troops panic and flee at the first shots. Only a daring night-time retreat across the East River saved the 9,000 strong Continental Army from total defeat.

Had Washington or his advisors known of the Synchronicity Code, he might have looked for another way to go in late August of 1776. The following timeline takes the interval from Washington's birth to his literal (if only partial) triggering of the French and Indian War and rolls it forward one time, *precisely* marking his first battle of the Revolutionary War:

George Washington

- **Born** February 22, 1732
-
-
- **50% Mark**: May 28, 1954 French and Indian War commences following Washington's imprudent actions in the Jumonville Affair *(Exact: May 26, 1754)*
-
-
- **Battle of Long Island:** August 27, 1776

This correlation is accurate to within two days over a span of 44 years.

* * *

How does one size up in one's own mind whether the Synchronicity Code is a real phenomenon or not? If your measure for whether it is real or not depends on statistical studies, then you must design those studies in such a way that captures the true nature of the phenomenon. It is a phenomenon that depends on the *meaning* of events, and favors coincidences. If you are careless about the meaning, the results will suffer.

American soldiers in the Battle of Long Island

Categories of Meaning

We are dealing with at least three categories of *meaning* in the timelines of the Synchronicity Code.

Category 1: Synchronicity. This is the where synchronicity points you to two events to use as a base to measure against. A prime example is the simultaneous death of Adams and Jefferson on July 4, 1826, which naturally refers back to the 4th of July in 1776 fifty years earlier to the day.

Category 2: Collective meaning that is important to a culture or civilization. Here the high points, such as beginning or ending dates of wars, appear amenable to mapping via the Synchronicity Code. Assassinations, especially ones that greatly move a nation or relate to wars, qualify as well. Classic Jungian synchronicity may well play a role here (and in Category 3 below) too. An example of this shown in Chapter 8 is the many parallel coincidences that accompany the Lincoln-Kennedy assassination timeline.

Category 3: *Individual meaning.* Here we are in our most subjective territory, and thus the least reliable from a statistical and evidentiary perspective, because it necessitates that we try to go inside the heart and soul of an individual to ferret out what is most important to him or her. In cases like Washington's, we may take the correlations that the Synchronicity Code provides us with as guides in search of the right meaning.

* * *

The other day my brother raised an interesting question. It is all well and good to see timelines that show significant correlations. But how do we deal with the timelines that *don't* work? The first point is that the Synchronicity Code obviously requires some skill and experience to be applied properly. So a timeline that doesn't seem to work may be because you don't have a clue what you are doing (and that includes me!). Second, the ones that don't work may be ones where the true meaning lies elsewhere than where you presumed. This would be the case if we focused on George Washington's presidency instead of his military roles.

Third, sometimes the resolution of a Code sequence lies in the future and you can only realize it when you get there.

Fourth, I don't think it is reasonable to expect that correlations will be found every time you look for one. If this theory is true, a pretty profound law of nature is at work. There are no doubt nuances to the way events unfold across time. For myself, I feel I have barely scratched the surface of understanding what this means or whether there are exceptions to the rule.

Fifth, except in instances of triangulation discussed in the next chapter where only one Mark is focused on, a particular Code sequence need not be fulfilled at a particular TimeMark. Other dates down the line may be the ones that hit the Mark.

Nevertheless, I think my brother's question was designed to get at the fact that skeptics will take examples of apparent failures as proof that the theory doesn't work. I think this is fair only if the statistical sample can be designed to take into account the synchronicities that point the way. So let me answer the question this way. In researching for this book, I sought out examples, and this book is filled with them, of famous coincidences that involved measurable time intervals. With at most one or two few exceptions, in each such case a clear Synchronicity Code Mark was hit.

* * *

Jungian synchronicity and the Synchronicity Code are woven from the same cloth. So I want to ask you a question.

Based on your own life experience up until this point, do you believe, as Jung believed, that synchronicity is a real phenomenon, or are meaningful coincidences just quirky accidents that are bound to happen amongst the near infinite number of events that are constantly happening all the time?

If you believe that synchronicity is real, then it is no stretch at all to consider the Synchronicity Code as a real phenomenon. The phenomena can be thought of as a subset of synchronicity that deals with numerical coincidences. While a subset, it has special qualities:

1. Unlike synchronicity, in which two events usually occur at the same time, the Synchronicity Code applies to a series of three or more events which necessarily take place across time.

2.   When events are linked by simple divisions of time, or by the Power of Ten, these numerical patterns may be viewed as synchronous phenomenon in and of themselves. Number itself becomes a type of meaningful coincidence.

3.   The Synchronicity Code allows one to approach synchronous events from a quasi-causal vantage point. It allows for "if-then" analysis: if these two meaningfully related events occur, then we can look for a third event in the series.

4.   The Synchronicity Code can potentially be approached statistically, so long as you base your studies on where the meaning lies. The examples in this chapter illustrate this point: we were able to find statistical relevance (although with a small sample size) when we started with coincidences involving July 4, 1776. We would not likely be so successful if we looked for timeline hits using the inauguration dates of all the American presidents, since there is no coincidence marker involved.

5.   There are cases where synchronicity relates to prophetic experiences. In contrast, the Synchronicity Code implicitly projects TimeMarks into the future which can be predictive.

6.   Through the Synchronicity Code, it is possible to view synchronous phenomenon in light of the wisdom of ancient cultures, in which number plays a foundational role. This

qualitative role to number has been lost to *quantitative*, statistics-based science, but could be regained.

7.　　The Synchronicity Code brings a further new element into the mix, that of *time gnosis*. What would it mean to individually or collectively *know* that a future event is likely to occur at a specific juncture or junctures in time?　In particular, could a widely publicized knowing of a possible adverse future event affect its outcome in positive ways?

It is important to find out.

From another perspective, rather than the Synchronicity Code being a subset of synchronicity, synchronicity could be thought of as a subset of the Synchronicity Code.　In other words, synchronicity occurs as a building block of how events unfold across time and into the future, as mapped by the Synchronicity Code.　This would explain why the best cases of the Synchronicity Code usually include meaningful coincidences.

As we proceed, bear in mind that the strongest statistical evidence in support of the Synchronicity Code comes up in three ways:

I.　　*Triangulation*:　where two or more related Synchronicity Code sequences converge and yield only one possible future date that rectifies the two lines, it becomes more likely that the correlation was not just random chance;

II.   *Precision:* As has been pointed out, it is one thing when you use a yearly TimeMark (+/- one year = "width" of 2 years) over the span of, say, a 70 year life span. It is another when the level of precision jumps up to another level, such as within one month, one week or even one day, +/-. For example, if there were 7 predetermined TimeMarks (as we often utilize), each a width of 2 years over a 139 year period, then you would have a 7 x 2 = 14/139 or about a 1 in 10 chance that the hit was random. But if those same 7 Marks were limited to one month of the relevant date, then you would have 14 in 139 x 12 = 1 in 120 chance that the hit was purely random. As we will later see, such a sequence occurred in the first 3 major wars fought by America. This might have led the astute observer of the Synchronicity Code to deduce, on June 29, 1914, that "this could get ugly".

III.   *Prediction:* If the Synchronicity Code can predict a future event, this would be the *sine qua non* of statistical evidence. The Synchronicity Code postulated a single date, in advance of its occurrence, to expect a "surprise attack" event on or about March 27, 2010. This turned out to be within one day of the precise date of March 26, 2010, when North Korea sunk a South Korean ship by torpedo.

7

TRIANGULATING
TIMELINES

If the triangles made a god, they would give him three sides. Charles de Montesquieu

I always liked Jill, from the first time I met her. We travelled out to Santa Barbara for her wedding to Jack, my high school buddy. Most of the weekend was a blur. Alas, their marriage was not to last. Fortunately for Jack, he's found someone else (happily whom I also like).

I first realized the significance of triangulation when I was emailing Jack about the scheduled date for his upcoming second wedding. Since Jack had been married once before, I thought it might be interesting to see if the proposed wedding date corresponded to the Synchronicity Code, using his birth date and the date of his first wedding as the two other dates. It did indeed correspond. It was interesting enough that here was a future date that had not yet happened that was "in tune" with the Synchronicity Code. But then it occurred to me to check the date of Jack's divorce. Sure enough, it too hit a Mark on the timeline of Jack's life. Then the obvious question arose, if all this was true for Jack, could it be possible that Jill would also show a correspondence? But how could this be? After all, Jack's birth date was different from Jill's, so her calculation would have to be unique to her, yet somehow also match Jack's. In fact, that is what I found. Jack's timeline utilized a 1.5 expansion of his birth—first wedding time span and Jill's timeline utilized 1.618, resulting in a match on the date of their divorce. The concept of triangulation, as applied to the Synchronicity Code, was born. Two independent timelines, with their own set of TimeMarks, aligning at specific intervals; this was the new concept. The possibility of reducing through triangulation the number of possible Marks for an expected future event was intriguing.

If two related but different Synchronicity Code sequences both correctly show a hit for a single significant event, this would be evidence of the validity of the Synchronicity Code, for the statistical likelihood of this happening by chance is twice as remote.

What follows is a small study of Founding Father presidents and their wives using the concept of triangulation. It moves us toward a possible approach to statistical analysis. Again, the sample size is small, so it is not intended as a formal proof. In this study, there are no coincidences, per se, involved, which I think makes it a little more hit or miss. But there is meaning—the meaning of one's choice of a significant other to spend one's life with. The timelines show the birth and death dates of the Founding Presidents and their wives and then shows when their wedding dates matched a TimeMark. For the purpose of this study, I have limited the possible Marks to five: 1/3, .382, 1/2, .618 and 2/3, leaving out 1/4 and 3/4.

George Washington

- **Born** February 22, 1732
-
- .382 **Married** January 6, 1758 (*exact January 23, 1758*—only 17 days!)
-
-
-
-
- **Died** December 1799

George Washington   Martha Washington

<u>Martha Washington</u>

- **Born** June 2, 1731
-
-
-
- .382   **Married** January 6, 1758 (*exact July 18, 1758*)
-
-
-
-
-
- **Died** May 22, 1802

Both George and Martha were married on a Mark of their own timeline, so their timelines triangulate to their wedding date.

John Adams (2nd President)

- **Born** October 30, 1735
-
- **Married** October 25, 1764 (Closest is 1/3 Mark on January 25 1766, so it misses)
-
-
- **Died** July 4, 1826

John Adams

Abigail Adams

Abigail Adams

- **Born** November 11, 1744
-
- **Married** October 25, 1764 (Also misses)
-
-
-
- **Died** October 28, 1818

Neither John nor Abigail were married on a Mark between their birth and death dates.

    (This surprises me a bit. Adams may have been a contentious fellow, but he also appeared to be quite close to Abigail, despite being physically separated from her for years at a time. I would have guessed that their wedding dates would have triangulated.)

<u>Thomas Jefferson</u> (3rd President)

- **Born** April 13, 1743
-
- 1/3 Mark: **Married** January 1, 1772 (*exact: January 6, 1771*)
-
-
-
-
- **Died** July 4, 1826

Thomas Jefferson

Martha Jefferson

Martha Wayles Skelton Jefferson

- **Born** October 30, 1748
-
-
- 2/3 Mark: **Married January 1, 1772** *(exact May 28, 1771)*
-
- **Died** September 6, 1782

Both Thomas and Martha Jefferson were married within the tolerance of a Mark of their own timeline, so their timelines triangulate to their wedding date.

This doesn't surprise me. Thomas Jefferson was extremely close to his wife and deeply despondent upon her death.

James Madison (4th President)

- **Born** March 16, 1751
-
-
-
- 1/2 Mark: **Married** September 15, 1794 *(exact November 11, 1793)*
-
-
-
- **Died** September 6, 1782

James Madison   Dolley Madison

<u>Dolley Payne Todd Madison</u>

- **Born** May 20, 1768
-
-
- 1/3 Mark: **Married** September 15, 1794 *(exact June 7, 1795)*
-
-
-
-
-
- **Died** September 6, 1782

Again, each of James and Dolley Madison were married on a Mark of their own timeline, so their timelines triangulate to their wedding date.

James Monroe (5th President)

- **Born** April 28, 1758
-
-
- 1/2 Mark: **Married** February 16, 1786 *(exact April 11, 1786)*
-
-
- **Died** July 4, 1831

James Monroe

Elizabeth Monroe

Elizabeth Kortright Monroe

- **Born** June 30, 1768
-
- **Married** February 16, 1786 [Miss]
-
-
-
- **Died** September 23, 1830

Only James Monroe, and not his wife, was married on a TimeMark of his own lifespan.

Here are the lifespans for each presidential couple, and the chances of a random hit of the date of their wedding against their own life's timeline:

President &/or Wife	Life Span	Chance of random hit is less than
George Washington	67 years	1 in 6
Martha Washington	71 years	1 in 7
John Adams	91 years	1 in 9
Abigail Adams	74 years	1 in 7
Thomas Jefferson	83 years	1 in 8
Martha Jefferson	34 years	1 in 3
James Madison	85 years	1 in 8
Dolley Madison	81 years	1 in 8
James Monroe	73 years	1 in 7
Elizabeth Monroe	62 years	1 in 7
Total:	721 years	1 in 7

Seven individuals of the group of ten individuals were married on one of their timeline Marks. The probability of this happening purely by chance is already slim.

Where it gets *really* unlikely is when you focus only on the triangulation pairs. Three of the five presidential couples had both spouses hit a Mark. The chances of one of them doing so is on average a 1 in 7 chance. It is equally (on average) a 1 in 7 chance for their spouse to hit a Mark within his or her lifespan. But now the challenge is much more exacting. The second spouse must hit a Mark that also mathematically corresponds to the other spouse's Marks.

The following shows the dates on each presidential couples' timelines that lined up between husband and wife, and thus were possible for triangulation:

President & Spouse	1/3	.382	.5
George Washington	10/6/54	1/23/58	1/23/66
Martha Washington	2/3/55	7/18/58	12/1/66

For George and Martha Washington, their wedding date hit the .382 Mark on both of their timelines, due to the somewhat unique situation that Martha was born slightly earlier and died slightly later than George. Even so, only 3 of the 5 Marks corresponded so that they were within one calendar year of each other. This means that instead of having a 1 in 6 chance of scoring a matching Mark, George had only 3 2-year periods (remember, the span of a Mark is one calendar year either side of the exact date of the event), or 6 chances in 67 years of hitting a corresponding mark, about a 1 in an 11 chance.

The other two presidential pairs are even more unlikely.

President & Spouse	1/3	2/3
Thomas Jefferson	1/14/71	
Martha Jefferson		5/28/71

Martha Jefferson lived only 34 short years. Only one Mark of Thomas was within the span of one of Martha's Marks. The random chance of the Jeffersons triangulating their wedding date on a Mark of each of their timelines is less than 1 in 40.

President & Spouse	1/3	.5	2/3
James Madison		11/10/93	1/25/08
Dolley Madison	6/6/95	12/15/08	

Two Marks correspond between James and Dolley Madison. (Note the 6/6/95 Dolley Mark and the 11/10/93 James Mark were themselves more than 1 year apart, but their wedding on September 15, 1994 was within the one-year tolerance of each.). The random chance of the Madisons triangulating the date of their wedding is less than 1 in 20.

Combining the 3 pairs, the random chance of this triangulation happening by pure chance is Washington 1/11 x Jefferson 1/40 x Madison 1/20 = well, lets just say it is very slim.

One important point about the triangulation of events is that the exacting nature of the mathematical pattern makes it unlikely that the Synchronicity Code sequence will match to the exact day. In instances when you find triangulation that is extremely accurate, I would consider that, rather than there being two (or more) unrelated timelines which correspond to one event, you may have one rolling cycle that continues hitting Mark after Mark.

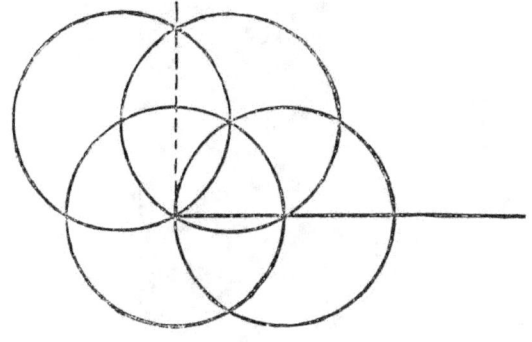

8

ASSASSINATIONS

Only when the clock stops does time come to life.
William Faulkner

Archduke Franz-Ferdinand died for love.

His wife Sophie, a Czech countess, was considered by Austria-Hungarians to be of lower social standing than the Archduke, so she was not permitted to publicly share in recognition of his rank in the royal court, nor even sit at his side at official events. One exception to this rule was when Ferdinand was surveying the troops in a military capacity. So, Ferdinand contrived to inspect the army in Bosnia, really for the purpose of permitting his wife to ride beside him in open carriage through the streets of Sarajevo.

Big mistake.

Franz Ferdinand and Countess Sophie Chotek

Early in the day on June 28, 1914, the Archduke's motorcade was bombed in an attempted assassination plot by Serbian conspirators. The unsuccessful attack wounded many bystanders, but the royal targets survived. Visibly shaken but unhurt, the Archduke and Duchess decided to continue on to attend the reception at the town hall as previously planned. Later, they again proceeded in their open car through the streets of Sarajevo to go to the hospital to visit victims of the earlier attack. But as chance (!) would have it, one of the "Black Hand" conspirators, Gavrilo Princip, happened to be standing in front of a café along the route traveled by the royal car and noticed Ferdinand's driver reversing after having made a wrong turn near Latin Bridge. Princip approached the car and fired two shots, one hitting the Archduke in the jugular vein and the other piercing the Duchess Sophie in the abdomen. As they sped toward the Governor's residence, Ferdinand pleaded with his wife, "Sophie, Sophie! Don't die! Live for our children!" He was pronounced dead on arrival, and Sophie died a few minutes later.

* * *

Without awareness of the Synchronicity Code, it would not be imagined that the Sarajevo assassination could in any way relate to the assassination of Abraham Lincoln 49 years earlier. But these pivotal events are mathematically linked across time, as we will show.

With his allegiance to the South, John Wilkes Booth originally planned to kidnap Lincoln, hold him hostage and force the Union to resume its policy of exchanging prisoners of war with the South. He imagined that the release of prisoners would re-fill the ranks of the depleted Southern army and lead to a resurgence of the war effort. But after attending a speech by Lincoln outside the White House in which Lincoln publicly supported the idea of giving the vote to black people, Booth changed his plan. Together with his co-conspirators, he would assassinate Lincoln, Secretary of State Seward and other top officials. This would be the inspiration to resurgence that the South needed.

On April 14, 1865, Lincoln and First Lady Mary Todd Lincoln attended the performance of Our American Cousin at the Ford Theatre. Major Henry Rathbone and his fiancé Clara Harris joined them. Booth knew well both the theatre building and the play, and at just the right moment of expected audience laughter, he rushed in and shot the President at the back of the head. Lincoln slumped over in his chair.

Rathbone tried to prevent Booth's escape and suffered severe knife wounds at the hands of the assassin. As Booth leapt from the balcony, his riding spur caught a flag adorning the box and he fell into the audience below, fracturing his foot as he landed. He made his escape on horseback only to be tracked down days later by Union soldiers at Garrett Farm. Booth was mortally wounded in the ensuing shoot-out.[18] Lincoln died within hours of the shooting. Secretary of War Edwin Stanton, who assumed control during the intervening hours, said upon Lincoln's passing, "Now, he belongs to the ages." One could also say with respect to the Synchronicity Code, that the ages belonged to him, for the meaning of Lincoln and his assassination did not end there. The tragic moment played itself out again and again, with different actors, but in similar dramas.

* * *

History is a relentless master. It has no present, only the past rushing into the future. John F. Kennedy

The duration of time in years between the assassinations of Lincoln in 1865 and Archduke

---

[18] There is some speculation that the killing of Booth was a staged event to appease a devastated nation and that Booth lived on for many years afterward, but that is beyond the scope of our present study.

Ferdinand in 1914 is 49 years. When you add 49 years to 1914, the year you get is 1963.

The Ferdinand assassination occurred at the half-way mark between the assassinations of Abraham Lincoln and John F. Kennedy.[19]

Lincoln-Ferdinand-Kennedy Assassinations

- **Lincoln killed** April 15, 1865
-
-
-
-
- 1/2 Mark: +49 years: **Archduke Ferdinand killed** June 28, 1914 *(exact midpoint: August 4, 1914—less than 6 weeks from the actual date)*
-
-
-
-
- +49 years: **JFK killed** November 22, 1963

Most people who are 50 years or older remember exactly where they were when they learned that President

---

[19] Note that the exact number of days between the assassinations of Lincoln and Kennedy is 36,014—very close to the large Power of Ten number 36000. This is anecdotal, but my impression is that this kind of number-count synchronicity plays a role in the Synchronicity Code phenomenon.

Kennedy had been shot. The sequence of events, starting with the President's motorcade as it made its way down Elm Street in Dallas, has been examined and re-examined over the years. Was there a lone gunman? Were there two shots or three shots? Was there a man up on the grassy knoll?

Theories will continue to come forth, some closer to the truth, some further. If the Synchronicity Code suggests anything, it is that, at the very least, the question of conspiracy *belonged* in the air. Both Lincoln and Archduke Ferdinand were killed in conspiracies involving multiple conspirators.

In keeping with our "follow the coincidences" rule, the parallels in the circumstances of Lincoln and Kennedy, and their killers, are extensive and well known among coincidence buffs. With the "hindsight" of the Synchronicity Code, these coincidences can be seen as something more. They are trace elements of how events are mapped across time.

Kennedy was elected to Congress in 1946. Lincoln was elected to Congress 100 years earlier, in 1846. Kennedy was elected President in 1960, Lincoln in 1860. Lee Harvey Oswald was born in 1939, Booth in 1838 (-1). Archduke Ferdinand was born in December 1863, only slightly more than a year before Lincoln's death and within a month of the death of Kennedy, a hundred years later. Both Kennedy and Ferdinand were riding in open motorcades when they were shot, and all three leaders were seated next to their wives at the time of the attacks. All three were felled by bullets shot by men in their early twenties.

Knowing as you now do of the Synchronicity Code link between Lincoln and Kennedy, would it surprise you to learn that the body of Kennedy was carried through the streets of Washington D.C. in the same carriage that carried Lincoln? (Such is the case.)

That Archduke Ferdinand was assassinated at the half-way point in time between the assassinations of Lincoln and Kennedy by itself proves nothing. What is significant is that *I was looking for one thing only: a major assassination* at a significant TimeMark, expecting to find something. That is different from accidentally finding the division at the 50% Mark and then claiming that this must somehow be a part of a patterning to events. The theory preceded the fact.

Over and over, the Synchronicity Code reveals a meaningful, repetitive pattern to events taking place across the span of time. This *is* inexplicable. Yet example after example points to a heretofore unrecognized truth about the way life unfolds:

When matters.

* * *

Future researchers will, it is hoped, become skilled at following the veins of meaning by comparing events occurring at each juncture along a timeline. For one thing, I am hoping they come to understand *why* Austria and the U.S. are linked by the above timeline. I have not yet found the link. But I think it is there to be found, and I think the Mayerling Incident is part of the puzzle.

The Mayerling Incident.

The 50% Mark between Archduke Ferdinand's birth in on December 18, 1863 and his death in 1914, is March 23, 1889. That date is about seven weeks from the date of the mysterious incident at Mayerling in Austria, on January 30, 1889.

History records this event as an apparent murder-suicide of Crown Prince Rudolf of Austria and his mistress Baronness Mary Vetsera. But there are factual inconsistencies that call this into question, which are discussed below. Prince Rudolf was the only son of Emperor Franz Josef I of Austria, and upon his death the line of succession moved to Franz Josef's brother, Karl Ludwig. But Ludwig soon renounced his succession rights, leaving his son, none other than *Franz Ferdinand*, the next heir apparent. Thus it was that the Mayerling Incident directly figured in the course of world history, without which Archduke Ferdinand would never have been heir presumptive to the Austro-Hungarian throne, and presumably, would then not also have been a coveted target of assassination by the Black Hand conspirators.

Ferdinand born—Mayerling Incident—Ferdinand
Assassination

- **Ferdinand born** December 18, 1863
-
-
-
- 1/2 Mark: **Mayerling Incident** January 30, 1889
  (exact midpoint: March 23, 1889)
-
-
-
- **Ferdinand killed** June 28, 1914

The incident took place at Rudolf's hunting lodge
in Mayerling. At the time, Prince Rudolf was married to
Princess Stephanie of Belgium, but he and the princess
were not believed to be close and the Prince was known
to have affairs with other women. Baronness Vetsera
was only 17 when she met the Prince in late 1888 and she
apparently quickly developed an almost fanatical
adoration for him. The similarities between the situations
that both Vetsera and Archduchess Sophie found
themselves in are worth remarking upon; both Prince
Rudolf and Archduke Ferdinand were with women at the
time of their death that for one reason or another, were
not allowed to be seen as equals with their men in the
royal court, and in both cases, the question of the
disapproval of Emperor Franz Joseph was in the air.

Baronness Vetsera, 1888

It is also interesting that conspiracy theories swirl around the deaths of Vetsera and Rudolf, thus placing the incident within meaningful context of the Lincoln-Ferdinand-Kennedy multi-actor conspiracies, in fact or conjecture. While it is increasing unlikely, with each passing year, that the truth of what happened at Mayerling (or for that matter, the Lincoln or Kennedy assassinations) will ever be fully known, a number of factual inconsistencies fuel the debate as to whether suicide was involved at all.

A cover-up was attempted right after the deaths. It was claimed that Rudolf died of heart failure and Vetsera's body was secreted away and not even mentioned. This was quickly called into doubt, however, and the official story changed to one of Rudolf's suicide, resulting from Rudolf's "mental imbalance". The story was that the two lovers had carried out a suicide pact after Franz Joseph demanded they separate. Whether or not true, this mirrors the impasse between Franz Joseph and Archduke Ferdinand in Ferdinand's insistence upon the right to marry Sophie, despite her inferior status in court. This version of the story has some credence; why make something like this up? On the other hand, why disguise a possible murder as a suicide? It is here that the Synchronicity Code invites comparison to other events in the timeline.

There is some speculation that a cover-up of the Kennedy assassination, if indeed there was one, was motivated by legitimate, even patriotic purpose, particularly on the part of Bobby Kennedy. In 1963, if it had been concluded that the Soviets were behind the shooting, then World War III and nuclear devastation could have been the result. By analogy, the Austro-Hungarian Royal Court may have considered it far better to risk the humiliation of "mental imbalance" than to risk political destabilization.

That a political conspiracy may have been behind the deaths of the Prince and his lover is predicated upon the following:

1.   Empress Zita of Austria, the last surviving crowned head from World War I, claimed throughout her life that the Crown Prince was *murdered*. She apparently believed that the Prince had been approached by French sympathizers to participate in the de-throning

of his pro-German father. Either he was killed by Austrian security officials, because the Prince was not so pro-German, or by French agents because he refused to carry out their plan and had to be silenced.

2.   The affair between Vetsera and Prince Rudolf was apparently an open secret in the Imperial Family. Thus, the idea that the love-crossed Prince took his and his beloved's life based on the Emperor's demand that the brand new couple separate was questionable, especially since Prince Rudolf was already a known womanizer.

3.   Major discrepancies exist between the claimed manner of the deaths and the factual evidence. The gun which killed the Prince did not belong to him. Six shots were fired from the weapon, but the initial report said that only one shot was fired. One shot, two shots, six shots, this would be the kind of thing that experts weighed in on when it came to Kennedy's assassination.

4.   The 1915 book, <u>The Secrets of the Hohenzollerns</u> written by Dr. Armgaard Karl Graves, who claimed to have been a German spy, also asserted that Prince Rudolf was assassinated because he did not support powerful Prusso-Germanic interests. His story is that three intruders, their faces covered, approached the royal hunting lodge as the Prince, the Baronness and two other trusted

companions, Max and Otto K, finished supper. The Prince was bludgeoned to death with a champagne bottle from the table, the Baroness, hysterically screaming at this point, was shot point blank in the head with a Stutzen (a short-barreled hunting gun). Recalling the survivable knife-wounds of Major Rathbone in the Lincoln assassination, Otto K was left for dead after being stabbed with a Hirsch-fanger (hunting dagger) between his shoulders. But he alone managed to survive. He pinned a note to his dead brother's clothes describing what had happened and then likewise disappeared into the night, for the consequences of witnessing the royal massacre, and living to tell about it, was likely to have been highly unfavorable to him, either from within the royal court itself or by further act of the perpetrators. He was said to have escaped to live in exile in America.

Triangulating Garfield

There have been other assassination attempts of American presidents other than Lincoln and Kennedy, and they were successful in the cases of Garfield and McKinley. As it turns out, in the case of Lincoln-Garfield, the resulting timeline is extraordinary.

President James Garfield   Charles Guiteau

James Garfield was shot by Charles Guiteau, who was apparently disgruntled after being refused for a civil service position, I would say a bit of an over-reaction! The shooting took place on July 2, 1881, but Garfield lingered and steadily worsened until he died on September 19, 1881. 6002 days separate the deaths of Lincoln and Garfield. This is again close to a large Power of Ten number, and invites the hypothesis that some kind of number synchronicity is at work that should be followed. (See also Footnote 19 above.) When we do so, by rolling the interval forward, we get the following dates:

April 14, 1865 Lincoln Assassination

September 19, 1881 Garfield death

February 24, 1898

August 2, 1914 *Within 5 weeks* of the **assassination of Archduke Ferdinand**

January 7, 1931

June 14, 1947

November 19, 1963 *Within 3 days* of the **assassination of John F. Kennedy**

April 25, 1980

September 30, 1996

March 7, 2013

The link is *undeniable*. Kennedy died within 3 days of the exact Mark! Nearly a hundred years after Lincoln! Ferdinand's death occurred within 5 weeks of the Mark on the Lincoln-Garfield line, over a similar span of time. While there is no way to definitively rule out that these links across time occurred just by chance, even the skeptic must at least pause and think about how extraordinary this alignment is. Sure it *could* be "just coincidence". But is it?

Armed with nothing but the dates of these prior events, it would have been possible to triangulate, *in advance,* the Lincoln-Garfield line with the Lincoln-Ferdinand line and come very close to the date of Kennedy's assassination. This does *not* mean that you could have predicted with certainty that Kennedy was going to be assassinated. But the timeline correlation might have given cause for grave concern.

The Twenty-year Presidential Jinx

Many readers are aware of the Twenty-year Presidential Jinx, also known as the Curse of Tippecanoe, and alternatively as Tecumseh's Curse. According to legend, every American president who was elected into office in a year beginning with zero would die in office. This held true from the time of William Henry Harrison (elected in 1840) up through John F. Kennedy (elected in 1960), until the pattern was finally broken by Ronald Reagan, who narrowly escaped the curse after being shot by John Hinckley, Jr. in 1981.

The reason this is called the Curse of Tippecanoe arises out of William Harrison's victory over Chief Tecumseh in a battle at Tecumseh's village alongside Tippecanoe River, earning him the nickname "Old Tippecanoe". The armed conflict started in the first place because, while governor of the Indiana territory, Harrison essentially duped the Indians into treaties that took unfair advantage of them, and this triggered a violent backlash. Upon Tecumseh's death in 1813 at the hands of Harrison's army, it is reported that Tecumseh's shamanic brother Tenskwatawa (also known as the Prophet) said the following:

> "Harrison will die I tell you. And when he dies you will remember my brother Tecumseh's death. You think that I have lost my powers. I who caused the sun to darken and Red Men to give up firewater. But I tell you Harrison will die. And after

118

him every Great Chief chosen every 20
years thereafter will die. And when each
one dies, let everyone remember the death
of our people."

So that's the curse. And I have no traffic with it,
other than to wonder why Tenskwatawa waited from
1813 until 1841 to take out Harrison. Now granted, in
order for the curse to come true, Harrison first had to be a

President William Harrison

"Great Chief", so he couldn't die until he was elected.
But once in office, Harrison has the distinction of having
the shortest presidency ever, dying one month after he
was inaugurated.

Tenskwatawa   Possible portrait of Tecumseh

The 20-year Presidential Jinx fits well with a Synchronicity Code timeline that hits all the big presidential dates, but, strangely enough, also links it to some of the key American armed conflicts.

As it is always best to start by "following the coincidences", the closest thing we have to a coincidence in this instance is the Garfield-McKinley pairing of assassinations, which were just 4 days shy of exactly 20 years apart (using death dates, not dates when the presidents were shot). By taking this interval and rolling it back 100 years (5 times) from the 1881 Garfield Mark, you get October 18, 1781, *one day before armed combat in the Revolutionary War ended with the British surrender at Yorktown.* Maybe that's just an accident, but I don't think so.

Let's pause. Isn't this mixing apples and oranges? Bringing in armed conflicts would seem to have nothing to do with the deaths of Presidents elected into office every 20 years, per the curse.

You'll see that there is more to the armed conflict link than just Yorktown. But this is good question, and this time I do not have a good answer for you. What can be seen, in this timeline and elsewhere, is that assassinations often go hand in hand with significant war events. Also, for purposes of the Synchronicity Code, beginnings and endings of wars seem to be interchangeable. Thus, Lincoln is assassinated at the end of the Civil War, Ferdinand at the beginning of World War I, and arguably Kennedy around the beginning of the Cold War (and certainly close to the very serious failed Bay of Pigs invasion or the Cuban Missile Crisis). But to quell any doubt that a link between armed conflict (especially beginnings and endings of wars) and the 20-year curse cycle, one just needs to look at the timeline. So many major events easily find their place in line. Is the Synchronicity Code really in evidence, weaving together many of the violent moments of American history over seven generations and counting?

It seems that it is.

October 19, 1781 Revolutionary War fighting ends with British surrender at Yorktown (exact hit within one day)

1801?

1821?

April 4, 1841 William Henry Harrison dies

April 12, 1861 Start of Civil War. *That's a major war event, just like the surrender at Yorktown..*

September 19, 1881 James Garfield dies (assassinated)

September 14, 1901 William McKinley dies (assassinated)

1921 In 1923, Warren Harding dies in office, fulfilling Tecumseh's curse. (This is not considered to have matched a Synchronicity Code Mark.)

December 7, 1941 Pearl Harbor. That's a direct hit on the start of World War II for the United States.

April 14, 1961 Failed Bay of Pigs invasion (Note that this is almost exactly 100 years from the start of the Civil War)

March 30, 1981 President Reagan assassination attempt

September 11, 2001 World Trade Center and related terrorist attacks (Note that this date was almost exactly 100 years from McKinley's death.)

2021???

Generally the dates congregate either around April or around September/October. The fact that *all* of the dates don't hit within a couple of days of precise Marks should not detract from your appreciation of this timeline. One of the reasons that I am not bothered by this is that we already know that many of these events are crisscrossing (triangulating) other Synchronicity Code timelines. God truly must be a mathematician to pull any of it off.

Note by the way that the above timeline is far more precise than the 20-year presidential curse itself, because each of the hits in this cycle is at most a few months, and as close as one week, from an exact match to the Garfield/McKinley base dates, whereas the presidential curse only requires that the president die within the 4-year term of the year he was elected.

Boston Massacre, March 5, 1770

9
TIMES OF WAR

What is human warfare but just this; an effort to make the laws of God and nature take sides with one party.
Henry David Thoreau

There have been only four really big wars involving the United States: the Revolutionary War, the

124

Civil War, World War I and World War II. Here the Synchronicity Code hits are so clear as to be hard to dismiss.

The First Triad of U.S. Wars

- 1775: **Revolutionary War begins**
-
-
-
-
- .618 Mark: 1861: **Civil War begins**
-
-
- 1914: **World War I begins**

The Civil War falls on the .618 Mark between the Revolutionary War and WWI. Conservatively speaking, there is less than a 1 in 13 chance that this is a purely random event. That's consistent with many Synchronicity Code events—not likely if it happens over and over, but not impossible either.

However, this 1 in 13 probability is based on the middle date hitting within one year of a Mark. In actual fact, this timeline is much more accurate. Not only is the triad exact to the year, *it is accurate to within less than a month*. The Revolutionary War started on April 19, 1775 with the battles of Lexington and Concord. World War I commenced with the assassination of Archduke Ferdinand on June 28, 1914, putting the April 12, 1861 start date of the Civil War only 14 days from the exact Mark:

- **Revolutionary War begins** April 19, 1775
-
-
-
-
-
- .618 Mark: **Civil War begins** April 12, 1861 *(exact Mark April 26, 1861, **14 days from a precise hit, over a period of 139 years.**)*
-
-
-
- **World War I begins** June 28, 1914

There are 1670 months between the start of the Revolutionary War and the start of the First World War. Working again with 7 possible internal Marks, and assuming a width of 2 units (+/- 1), here two months, this means that to score a hit the chances are 2 X 7 = 14 / 1670, or about 8 chances in a 1000 that this is a purely random occurrence. Since the hit was within 14 days, your width could have been only one month, which would make it 4 chances in a 1000.

The Second Triad of U.S. Wars

Once the first three U.S. wars hit a Mark, how likely do you think it would be that the next triad—the Civil War, WWI and WWII, would *also* fall on a Mark?

The challenge here is not to find a match using any old series of events, it is to find a match using *the next three major U.S. wars.* In this case WWI corresponds to the .66 (or 2/3rds) Mark, when America entered the war following Pearl Harbor in 1941.

- **Civil War begins** April 12, 1861
-
-
-
-
-
- 2/3rd Mark: **World War I begins** June 28, 1914 *(exact Mark: January 17, 1915)*
-
-
- **WWII begins for America**: December 7, 1941 ("A Day which shall live in infamy")

A Third Triad?

We don't yet know what history will label as the beginning of the next really big war. It is possible that the first Gulf War might be thought of as a start of a protracted engagement, inclusive of the 2001 invasion of Afghanistan and the 2003 invasion of Iraq, which may continue in various ways for decades. If so, the timeline is clear: the time span between the start of each world war rolled over two times hits the Persian Gulf War.

- **World War I begins** 1914
-
- 1/3rd Mark: **World War II begins** 1939
-
-
-
- **Persian Gulf War begins** 1989

I am personally not convinced that this marks World War III. But another possible timeline pointing to the future exists, which connects to a larger view.

- **World War I begins** 1914
-
- 1/4 Mark: **World War II begins** 1939
-
-
-
- **World War 3 begins** Circa 2014

This one worries me.

To understand why, we need to bring in the corollary principles of the Power of Ten and triangulation introduced in Chapters 5 and 7. The year 2014 lies on different, complex timeline which would triangulate with the 1914-1939-2014 line above, and this other multifaceted line unfolds according to the Power of Ten in 50 and 100 year leaps, which adds to the potential magnitude of the situation. I would even call this "the Primary Synchronicity Code Sequence of Major Wars of Modern Western Civilization."

Consider these years:

1714

1763

1814

1863 (1861-5)

1914

1963

2014

Three centuries ago, between 1701 and 1714 (note the end date), the War of Spanish Succession was fought among Spain, Great Britain, the Holy Roman Empire, the Dutch Republic, Portugal and others. While it is possible to go back further, let's consider this to be the starting place for the sequence.

Approximately 50 years later, 1763 marked the end of the Seven Years War, which was a truly global war involving all the major European powers and which played out in European, African, Indian, and North American theaters. The war was principally between the British Empire and the French and Spanish Bourbons.

Armies laid siege to forts, burned towns and fought across open fields. There was great loss of life.

About 50 years later, the Napoleonic Wars began in 1803 and ended in Napoleon's defeat at Waterloo on June 15, 1815. As I indicated earlier, the end is better measured from Napoleon's first abdication in April of 1814. This resulted from Napoleon's epic loss in the Battle of Leipzig in October of 1813, which was the largest, most deadly fight of 19th Century Europe. The Napoleonic Wars in general are notable in that they saw a significant enlargement in the size of armies and the consequent death toll.

Next, the American Civil War ran from 1861 to 1865 and is the deadliest war ever fought on American soil. In the Battle of Gettysburg alone early in July, 1863, 51,000 men died.

Half a century later, World War I began (as we've noted, the Synchronicity Code appears to mark beginnings and endings of wars interchangeably) with the assassination of Archduke Ferdinand on June 28, 1914.

1963 found the United States and the Soviet Union embroiled in the satellite war of Vietnam, but perhaps even more importantly, as evidenced by the Cuban Missile crisis, the two great world powers threatened each other and the rest of the world with mutual annihilation via atomic bombs. While no all out war erupted (except for Vietnam), no riskier time has existed before or since (thus far) for modern civilization. This raises an important point as we look to 2014 and beyond: the nature of warfare can change. We don't yet know what to expect as to the shape of weaponry in years to come.

The basic pattern is one of major wars ending or beginning around the 14th year of a century, as well as around the 63rd year, thus evidencing a steady periodicity of approximately 50 years. You may have noted that World War II does not fall on this cycle, but rather on its accent, as 1939 is 25 years or one-half the 50 year cycle from 1914. It thus (arguably) falls within the same broad, complex cycle, with the added significance that it allows for triangulation on a separate line to 2014. It is just this 25-year Mark that is the basis for the World War I— World War II interval that we started this discussion with, and sets up the Power of Ten structure. In other words, when you have a 25-year or 50-year pairing, always think 100, which points to 2014.

What if nothing happens in 2014, give or take a year? That would be nice. But does it prove the theory wrong? Not on this account. I can easily have it wrong. We are at the beginning of a new way of looking at time and history, where trial and error is the way forward.

Surprise Attacks

We opened this book with a brief description of the 9/11 timeline. When 9/11 occurred, references to the Japanese attack of Pearl Harbor began almost from the start. In both attacks, the acts of aggression became, for U.S. citizens, days "that will live in infamy". The transference of meaning from one event to the other suggested a possible pairing for Synchronicity Code analysis, which turned out to be true.

In looking at possible historical precedents, there is a possible link to a surprise terrorist attack against Tsar Alexander of Russia in 1881 (60 years before Pearl Harbor and 120 years before 9/11). But I do not find this compelling, as the event did not involve America, either directly or in its implications.[20] We must look further for implications of the Pearl Harbor-9/11 pairing.

Explosion of the USS Arizona's magazine at Pearl Harbor

---

[20] Nothing precludes the Synchronicity Code from crisscrossing the globe to weave its tapestry of events. While there is no hard and fast rule about which events are sufficiently related in meaning to belong to a given timeline, common sense is the guide. While a case could be made for it, I am inclined to discount the validity of the Tsar Alexander II incident as part of the 9/11 timeline. In contrast, a compelling case can be made for the inclusion of the assassination of Archduke Ferdinand in the Lincoln-Ferdinand-Kennedy timeline, as the latter marked the start of World War I and thus played an important roll in the course of U.S. history. Once we include the Ferdinand assassination, this opens the door to inclusion of the ancillary Synchronicity Code related to the Mayerling Incident in 1889. I don't know why U.S. and Austrian history is intertwined, but according to Synchronicity Code, it is.

In broad strokes, should a third infamous attack yet be due to occur in the future, these are the dates for our progeny to watch:

1.   1941 to 2001 = 60 x .33 = 20. 2001 + 20 = **2021**

2.   1941 to 2001 = 60 x .382 = 23. 2001 + 23 = **2024**

3.   1941 to 2001 = 60 x .5 = 30. 2001 + 30 = **2031**

4.   1941 to 2001 = 60 x .618 = 37. 2001 + 37 = **2038**

5.   1941 to 2001 = 60 x .66 = 40. 2001 + 40 = **2041**

Ah, I think, that last one has a ring to it. 1941 to 2001 to 2041. This sequence also expresses the Power of Ten. While one can't rule out the other Marks, I would watch 2041 in particular.   Or perhaps my grandson or granddaughter should do that for me.

The Surprise Attack Cycle

I vividly remember the first time the World Trade Center was attacked in 1993 because . . . I was on the 57th floor of One World Trade Center when it happened.

At the time I was an associate attorney at the law firm of Brown & Wood (which later merged with Sidley & Austin). It was around lunch time and I was talking on the phone with my wife.   Suddenly there was a thundering BOOM! and to my eyes (I was facing away from the window toward my office doorway) it looked like the floor shot up 2-3 feet and then down again. I tried to say something about what had happened but then…the phones went dead. Within less than a minute there was already smoke in our hallway and I knew we had to get out fast. As we walked down the stairwell, I was near a man who claimed that he worked for the building and that a transformer blew out on the 44th floor (so not to worry!) This was some comfort to me, for a little while. But then as we passed the 44th floor on the way down the stairs, the smoke was getting thicker, which should not have been the case if the building worker was correct. This is when I began to taste the fear of it. Some people around me were getting hysterical,

The World Trade Center, where the author worked in 1993

which oddly seemed to calm me down. Soon we began to see firemen walking past us as they climbed the stairs, wearing heavy clothing and gear. But what really struck me was that as we exited the building, a line of firemen had locked arms which required us to walk between them and the wall of the building until we reached the corner and safety. Shards of glass were showering down just beyond their heads as people broke windows up above. This act of bravery left such an indelible impression on me that to this day I get choked up every time I see a fireman.

Once one knows of the Synchronicity Code, one cannot think of the 1993 and 2001 World Trade Center events without immediately looking for a third meaningfully related event across time. That third event could lie in the future or in the past.[21] As I researched this, my mind was again drawn to Pearl Harbor, as it is the quintessential surprise attack in U.S. history and was frequently alluded to in the media during the aftermath of the 9/11 bombing. The link is there, but to find it one must "work backwards" from the two World Trade Center attacks.

Before we show the link to Pearl Harbor, there is another, related "timeline-within-the-timeline" that should first be presented. It is incredible to me, but difficult to dismiss by virtue of its precision. It relates to the Oklahoma City bombing.

---

[21]Note that locating a mathematically linked third event in the past does not preclude future links, since the timeline can clearly unfold in complex, multilayered ways.

The timeline for these events looks like this:

- **First World Trade Center bombing** February 26, 1993
-
- 1/4 Mark: **Oklahoma City bombing** April 19, 1995 (*exact April 17th*)
-
-
-
-
- **Second World Trade Center bombing** September 11, 2001

The striking thing about this timeline, and why it can't be ignored, is that the Oklahoma City bombing occurred on the 25% Mark between the two World Trade Center bombings. Eight years, six months and 16 days separate the two World Trade Center bombings, a total of 3119 days. One-quarter of this number is 780 days. 780 days added to February 26, 1993 is April 17, 1995. This is the day that Timothy McVeigh and Terry Nichols began loading their Ryder truck with explosives in Herrington Kansas, culminating in the bombing at 9:02 a.m. on the morning of the 19th. Accurate hits like this are strong evidence in support of the Synchronicity Code theory. The Oklahoma City bombing occurred within two days of the exact 1/4 Mark between the two World Trade Center attacks. Also, as lesser timelines tend to appear within larger Synchronicity Code sequences (the ancient philosophers' analogous expression for this is "wheels within wheels"), what we see as the 25% Mark on one timeline is often also the 50% Mark of a smaller timeline. Here, the conviction of Timothy McVeigh occurs on another Mark—*precise to within a week*. The Oklahoma City bombing, occurred a mere 2 days from the exact 50% Mark between the 1993 bombing and the day McVeigh was sentenced to death.

WTC – Oklahoma City – McVeigh Conviction – 9/11

- **First World Trade Center bombing** February 26, 1993
-
- 1/4 Mark: **Oklahoma City bombing** April 19, 1995 (*exact April 17th*)
-
- 1/2 Mark: **McVeigh sentenced to death** June 13, 1997
-
-
-
- **Second World Trade Center bombing** September 11, 2001

One can only speculate why these events are linked by the Synchronicity Code, apart from the obvious fact that they represent the most significant bombings on American soil in its nearly two and a half century existence. There may be more of a message in the connection left to be deciphered, but I leave that for another time.[22]

Wheels within wheels: finding a hidden cycle of the Synchronicity Code

The 1993 and 2001 World Trade Center bombings occurred eight and a half years apart and Pearl Harbor occurred about 60 years earlier. As I considered these events, at first I could not fathom how one might fit these dates into the Synchronicity Code, since 8.5 years would not hit any of my pre-set Marks, at .25, .33, .382, .5, .618, .75, nor even .80. Logically, the only thing left to try was to simply string 8.5 years together in a series, subtract from 1993 and see if there was a hit.

The results stunned me.

Here is the series based upon subtracting 8.5 years (the exact calculation was 3119 days) from September 11, 2001:

September 11, 2001

February 26, 1993

---

[22]The author is aware that conspiracy theorists have claimed that the Oklahoma City and World Trade Center attacks may in some way be connected, based in part on claimed phone records showing a possible link between Terry Nichols and Ramzi Yousef. I tend to view this link as a parallel, synchronous expression of the Synchronicity Code rather than a case of collusion. As another instance of meaningful coincidence, the Oklahoma City bombing occurred at 9:02 a.m., the South Tower of the World Trade Center was hit at 9?03 a.m.

August 13, 1984

January 29, 1976

July 16, 1967

December 13, 1958

June 17, 1950

December 2, 1941

What? Is this even possible? Pearl Harbor was attacked on December 7th 1941. The Synchronicity Code appeared to link this date to the two World Trade Center Bombings across a span of 60 years, precise to a mere few days. *But wait.* Maybe it is even more precise than this. The first World Trade Center attack back in 1993 occurred in the early afternoon, and the first plane hit on 9/11 at 8:46 a.m. So the actual duration is less than 3119 days. What if the series were determined by using the two outside dates and working back toward the middle? This would require a modest hourly adjustment of the fixed duration from 3119 days to 3118.3 days. Here is the same list of dates based on the hourly adjustment.

September 11, 2001

February 27, 1993

August 15, 1984

January 31, 1976

July 19, 1967

January 4 1959

June 21, 1950

December 7, 1941

Using the outside dates as the basis for the cycle, the Synchronicity Code thus links Pearl Harbor and September 11, 2001, over a span of 60 years. The previous 1993 bombing fits this cycle *to within 1 day*. This is amazingly precise. So much so that I would suggest that the sequence itself, inclusive of the sub-cycle involving Oklahoma City, to be the strongest evidence of the validity of the Synchronicity Code theory that has been uncovered to date. What are the chances that the Pearl Harbor—1993—2001 timeline would also triangulate with the 1993—Oklahoma City—2001 timeline, with such precision?

The combination seems wildly beyond chance.

One shouldn't move on from this timeline without at least checking whether any *other* meaningfully related events occurred on or about the dates between 1941 and 2001. Here is what we find:

<u>**September 11, 2001**</u>　　9/11 Attacks

February 27, 1993	World Trade Center Bombing (*exact date of bombing is February 26, 1993, -1 day*)
August 15, 1984	No known major world event involving surprise attack or U.S. affairs.[23]
February 1, 1976	12 Provisional Irish Republican Army bombs explode in the West End of London (*exact date of bombings is January 29, 1976, -3 days.*)
July 20, 1967	An explosion and fire aboard the U.S. Navy aircraft carrier *USS Forrestal* in the Gulf of Tonkin leaves 134 dead. (*exact date of incident is July 29, 1967, +9 days*)
January 5, 1959	On January 4, 1959 (*exact -1 day*), rebel troops led by Che Guevara and Camilo

---

[23]While no major event corresponds to this date, it is oddly amusing that on August 11, 1984, within 4 days of exact Synchronicity Code Mark, during a voice check for a radio broadcast, President Ronald Reagan joked, "My fellow Americans, I'm pleased to tell you today that I've signed legislation that will outlaw Russia forever. We begin bombing in five minutes". One could almost speculate that this gaffe was triggered by Synchronicity Code itself, for the sake of marking an important interval in the "surprise attack" cycle. This is merely anecdotal.

Cienfuegos enter the city of Havana in Cuba. The United States recognizes the Castro regime 3 days later.

June 23, 1950

North Korea invades South Korea in a surprise attack which marks the start of the Korean War (*exact date of attack is June 25, 1950, +2 days*). Two days later, President Truman orders U.S. Forces to aid in the defense of South Korea.

December 7, 1941

Pearl Harbor

If you are not yet seeing it, look at these dates and events again. The list includes a number of the most important surprise attacks conceivable during the last century. One after another. The complete timeline is so striking, so precise, so intricate that an entire book could be written about just this one Code sequence. We are faced with a preposterous situation. Either the sequence is pure chance, which is difficult in extremis to argue, or the sequence evidences a true case of the Synchronicity Code, which is preposterous in its implications for mankind.

If the complete surprise attack sequence is something *other* than pure chance (which is what I am claiming), then *we all have been missing* a tremendous force or principle dictating how life unfolds.

Nothing here has been "curve-fitted" to smooth out the data and make the fit appear as accurate as possible. The dates were fixed by the Synchronicity Code based on the Pearl Harbor—World Trade Center Bombing as the two outside dates. Either it fits or it doesn't. We can quibble about the significance of some of the lesser events (IRA bombings, Gulf of Tonkin fire) on the stage of history. But it is nothing short of amazing that the North Korean invasion fits this timeline to a tee. No other event in the decade following the end of World War II could have been more fitting. With respect to the Cuban Revolution, prior to the Synchronicity Code, I would not have thought of it this way, but the success of Castro's overthrow must also have been a shock (like a surprise attack) and it had major ramifications for the Cold War just a few short years later. These dates lock right into the Pearl Harbor—1993 Bombing—World Trade Center series, which already stands on its own as the pre-eminent case for the validity of the Synchronicity Code theory.

And the story doesn't end there….

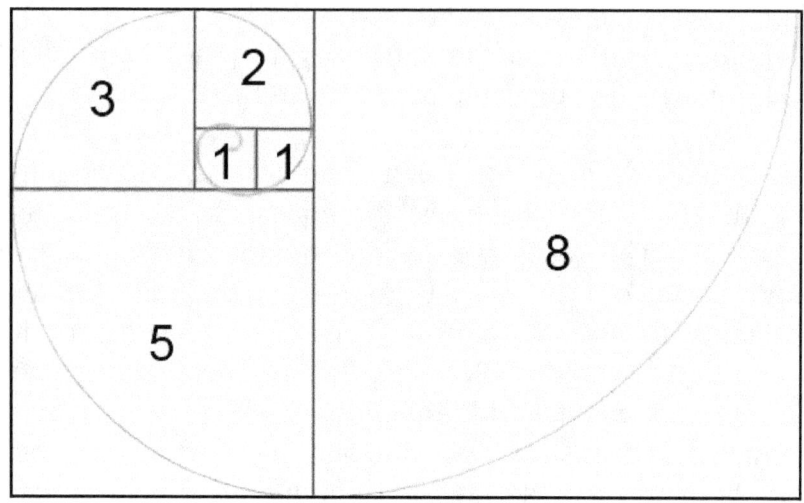

10

STOCK MARKET PANICS[24]

God ever geometrizes. Plato

It was late December, 2007. I looked up from my computer screen feeling awestruck. My wife, Martha was sitting across the study and I said, "the [stock market] top is in. It is now going to go down for months if not years and *virtually nobody knows this.*"   This recognition, that very few others in the world saw what I had just seen, was deeply moving to me. Something potentially very harmful was about to unfold. Yet there

---

[24] The trading and investing information in this book is solely for educational purposes and in no way should be construed as trading or investment advice.

was no one to tell, nothing to be done about it. Even if I tried to tell someone, they would think me crazy. History is riddled with prognosticators whose predictions fell flat on their face.

In its time dimension, the calculation behind this realization was quite simple. I took the high of 1987 and the high of 2000 and multiplied this time duration by the Fibonacci ratio of .618 to get September/October of 2007 on the monthly scale. Pure Synchronicity Code. This was also 100 years from the Panic of 1907. That's the Power of Ten. In addition, the 1987-2007 period was 20 years, which would have rolled back to 1907 as well. So there was triangulation.

My call was spot on.

Did I get rich from it? Um...er...well no I'm afraid not.

I went short right from the start. After the market tanked, I got too big for my britches. At the time, I felt I was pretty good at determining when a big move might be beginning, "finding alpha" as I called it, but I was still only guessing about the end of the trend, or "finding omega". In this case, I fully expected the market to go down for many many months. I made good money right out of the gate, mostly with IBM puts. But in the summer 2008, clever chap that I am, I thought I could *temporarily* reverse my position, ride the second wave up, and then get short again in time for the major third wave down.

BIG MISTAKE.

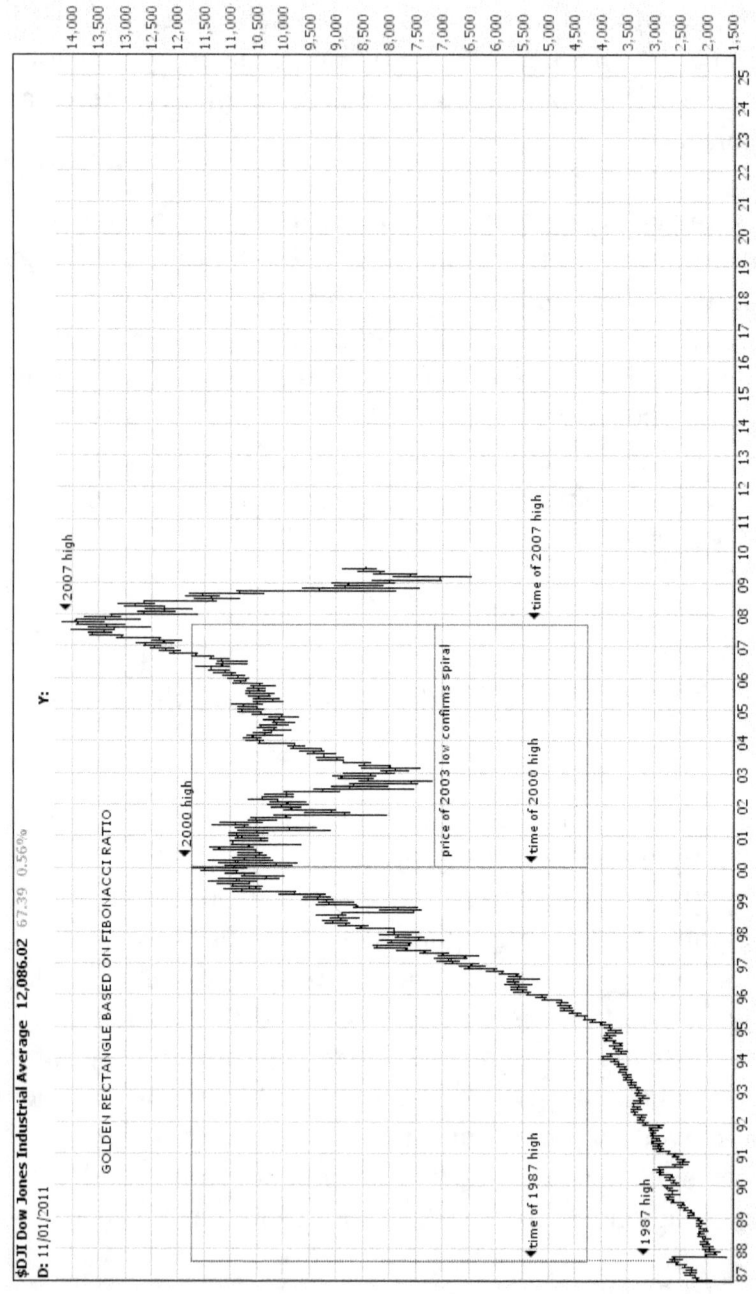

Instead, I got caught in the downdraft, along with everyone else, when wave two never materialized. From being up nearly 60% in July of '08, I found myself with a loss at the end of the year. It is true that I still "beat the Dow", as my losses were smaller than the market averages, but that was no consolation to a guy who thought he had it all figured out.

I felt a little bit like Icarus flying too close to the sun. Ouch.

Not one to give up easily. I kept up with my research into time and the geometry of the markets. From time to time I had conversations with one of my wife's dog training clients, who is a retired trader. He was very skeptical that market turning points can be predicted. It just so happened that on Sunday April 25, 2010, he asked me, with a hint of a smirk on his face, what my latest market prediction was. I said, "NOW. I am predicting a major turn in the market starting right now and continuing possibly for months." That was it.

My prediction was for a market top on April 26, 2010. What followed was the largest correction in the market since the 2009 lows, a correction that persisted until the end of June. So I call that a hit.

Of course, a casual conversation out in the middle of a field isn't exactly proof of anything. But in this case, my prediction was also in writing. Not only that, the underlying calculations for this call were first made by me *more than six months earlier*, and I have the evidence to back this up. On Thursday, September 24, 2009 at 2:11 p.m., I sent an email to a fellow trader which says, in relevant part:

> "The surprising part relates to one of my most valued rules, which says that if a low "locks in" in a certain way, the move off of that low can't end except at a specific future time junctures. The first such juncture is passed. *The next is April 26, 2010*, followed by September 20, 2010. This logically implies, I think, that any turn in the near future will not result in a direct resumption of the bear market into new lows. We may be facing a retrace of the current correction (like a Wave B), but the larger upward corrective move still may be in tact." (*Italics added*)

I will not go into the specifics of the calculations behind this forecast, but *something* was working in my theories. The chart on the next page shows a part of the geometric structure, consisting of a Fibonacci Golden Section that frames the time and price elements at play.

One of the reasons that predicting the markets is so difficult is that it usually ends up being a prediction about a prediction. With respect to the April 26, 2010 prediction, I was looking for the markets to resume the downmove that started in 2007. I took a fairly big position for the size of my account based on this view. For a while things were looking GREAT. I was right on in my timing. I called a turn to the day that then moved in my direction for *months*. Alas, I was not

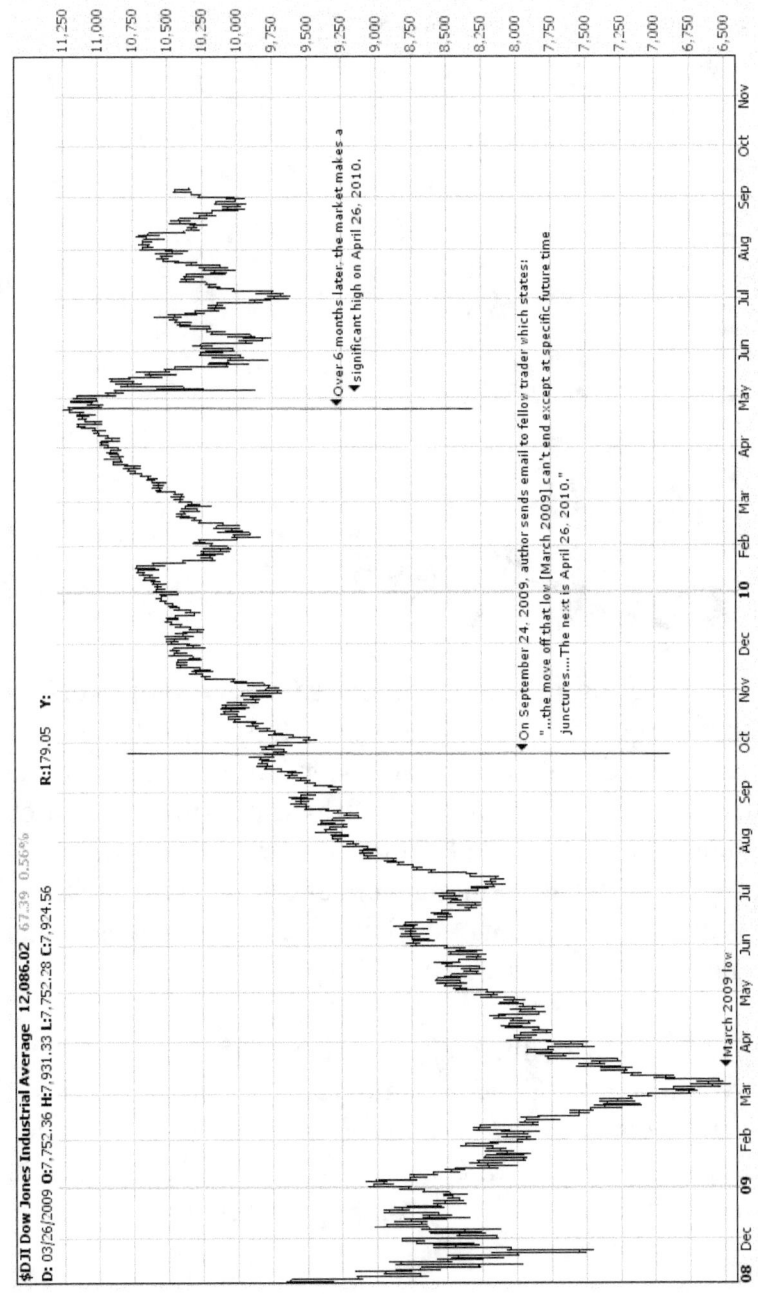

$DJI Dow Jones Industrial Average 12,086.02 67.39 0.56%
D: 03/26/2009 O:7,752.36 H:7,931.33 L:7,752.28 C:7,924.56   R:179.05   Y:

Over 6 months later, the market makes a
significant high on April 26, 2010.

On September 24, 2009, author sends email to fellow trader which states:
"...the move off that low [March 2009] can't end except at specific future time
junctures....The next is April 26, 2010."

March 2009 low

correct about the ultimate magnitude of the turn and the market broke to new highs seven months later. I took a hit on the trade.

It's an Icarus thing.

Predicting magnitude is not easy, in the markets or in current events. This is the same thing with the North Korean torpedo attack touched on in Chapter 6 and further discussed in Chapter 12. It was possible to predict that such a surprise attack might occur. But as of early spring 2011 what remains uncertain is the historic magnitude of the event. Will it be the first act in what becomes an all out war, or not?

A second point, both in terms of trading and with the Synchronicity Code generally, is that *perfect order doesn't mean perfect predictability.* Based on the configuration at the time, the market could have made a "perfect top" on April 26th, or September 20th, or some further date. It is not easy (though it may be possible) to know in advance which one.

Earlier in this book I alluded to the fact that my years of market research, which was the initial background that led to the discovery of the Synchronicity Code, has more to it than just a time component. Look at any stock chart and you see that time marches from left to right, on any time scale from one minute to one month per bar. Price on the other hand goes up and down vertically. The legendary trader and forecaster W.D. Gann postulated that time converts to price and price to time, which he called the "squaring of price and time". As an example of what he meant, if IBM topped out near the price of $120, as it did on July 13, 1999, you might look for a tradable turning point to occur 120 days later, as it did on December 31, 1999. The market didn't have to do this, just like the Synchronicity Code doesn't have to hit any particular Mark. But one might be wise to watch for it.

Or so Gann's theory goes.

Like the ancient philosophers who studied sacred geometry and sought to "square the circle," I believe the markets *square price and time by means of the circle*. It goes beyond the scope of this book to flush out what this is all about, but on the next page, I will give you a picture to show you what I mean. If you go looking for this phenomenon on a typical computer-generated chart, you won't find it, because proper structure depends on proper scaling of price to time.

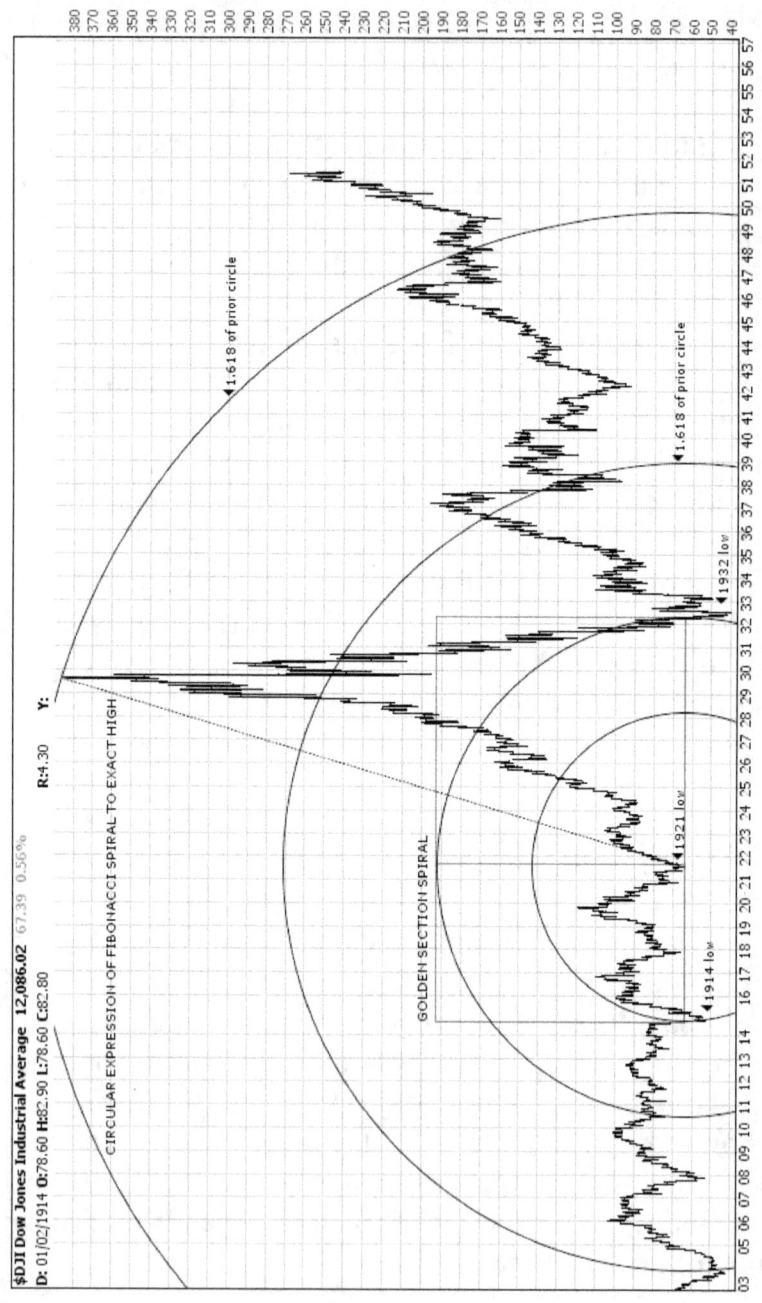

My tentative conclusions in applying the Synchronicity Code to the market follow.

1. In and of themselves, any two market turning points may or may not have a connection in terms of the meaningful coincidences that line this book. Nevertheless, consecutive tops, tops to bottoms, bottoms to tops, and bottoms to bottoms often "multiply" to pinpoint subsequent turning points based on time sequences related to the Synchronicity Code.

2. While successive highs and lows of the market can be thought of as "meaningfully related" events, absent some sort of coincidence, this may be somewhat hit or miss. Numeric coincidences, however, might be thought to occur at, say, double tops, turning points at matching anniversary dates, and turning points at a near-identical price to a prior recent turning point.

3. Many others have applied market forecasting techniques under the rubric of "technical analysis" that relate, directly or indirectly, to the mathematics of the Synchronicity Code. With the discovery of the Synchronicity Code, it may be possible to analyze meaningful coincidences in real world events affecting a stock or a company *outside* of these market charting techniques, and then look for convergences with signals generated through traditional technical analysis.

4.   Some market driven events, like the 1929 crash, are unique in that the markets themselves become news that affects the public at large, and thus can be linked to events outside the market via Synchronicity Code sequences. The primary example of this is the 1929-1939-1949 sequence discussed in Chapter 12.

5.   Perhaps the most significant point I would make in considering the Synchronicity Code in relation to the markets, is that the time element appears to be *only one dimension* of a more complex geometry that relates price to time and time to price. W.D. Gann pragmatically applied this with his discovery of the "squaring of time and price". R.N. Elliott, the developer of Elliott Wave Theory, also showed how the market often moves in waves governed principally by the Fibonacci ratio. In my view, the focus of research should be on circular calculations that expand and contract based on the Fibonacci ratio (they are often referred to as "Fibonacci Arcs" in computer tool sets). These are the missing link between Gann and Elliott. But as far as the Synchronicity Code is concerned, this leads one to ponder, if time is just one dimension of synchronous, mathematical patterning in the markets, it may also be just one dimension of world events outside the markets. What would it mean, then, to find the geometry of time—the vertical dimension if you will—in everyday events?

11

SYNCHRONICITY'S CLOCK

You're just jealous because the voices only talk to me.

Search "remarkable coincidences" on the internet and you will come across the following. On December 5, 1664, a ship sank in the Menai Strait off the coast of Wales. All 81 passengers died, except one man named Hugh Williams. 121 years later, *on December 5, 1785,* another ship sank in the same Strait in which all died but for one individual—named Hugh Williams! All this is strange enough, but as will not be surprising by now, things go in threes. On *December 5,* 1860, a small vessel again sank off the coast of Wales in the Menai Strait. All died except a man named Hugh Williams.

The Menai Strait

People tend to laugh when they hear about this coincidence, so outrageous it is. It totally strains credulity, which leads some to dismiss it out of hand. Somebody made it up, right? Perhaps, but up until now no one knew about the Synchronicity Code. So it is almost just as ridiculously impossible to find that the Synchronicity Code neatly weaves the dates together. 196 years separates the first sinking in 1664 and the last in 1860. The 1785 shipwreck occurs right on the .618 Mark:

The Shipwrecks Of Hugh Williams

- **First Shipwreck** December 5, 1664
-
-
-
-
- .618 Mark: **Second Shipwreck** December 5, 1785
-
-
- **Third Shipwreck** December 5, 1860

The number of days elapsed between the first and last shipwrecks is 71577. .618 of this is 44235 days, which falls on January 25, 1786. This is about 6 weeks from an exact hit over a span of nearly 200 years. Why the divergence? The synchronous anniversary date of December 5th appears to have "pulled" the exact daily count of the Synchronicity Code Mark.[25]

Skeptics have always been able to argue that amazing coincidences are just that...coincidences and nothing more. While nothing can convince one who refuses to be convinced, the Synchronicity Code lends powerful evidence that some "coincidences" are far from random occurrences.

They are part and parcel of the fabric of time.

* * *

I want to go ahead of Father Time with a scythe of my own. H.G. Wells

There are some well known cases of the paranormal, that seem to cross the barrier of time *and space*, which events appear to be confirmed, if not validated by the Synchronicity Code.

---

[25] We are only beginning to understand the "pushing" and "pulling" of Marks from exact correspondence. This example of anniversary dates is one example. The exacting requirements of triangulating two Synchronicity Code sequences (as in the wedding dates for two spouses) may be another.

Timeslip: Walking back into the past....

Sometimes a walk in the park is anything but.

On August 10, 1901, two Oxford professors, Anne Moberly and Eleanor Jourdain, were strolling in the garden of the Petit Trianon at Versailles when a strange shimmering effect occurred before their eyes. One moment they were walking in 1901, and the next they seemed to have been transported to an earlier time at the exact location they were standing. Passersby now were wearing 18th century clothing and wigs and appeared to be quite agitated. A repulsive man with pockmarked face approached them and urged them to head in another direction. As they followed him past a line of trees they heard strains of music and saw an aristocratic woman painting a water color.

Eventually the vision faded, but the incident was made even more dramatic when the women realized that the path they had walked was now blocked by an old stone wall. Upon their return to England, they researched the historical records and concluded that they had somehow been transported back in time to the day, August 10, 1792, in which the sacking of the Tuileries and massacre of the Swiss Guards had taken place[26]. The woman in the garden was none other than Marie Antoinette. The professors were so struck by this that they wrote a lengthy manuscript describing their

---

[26] It is said that Napoleon witnessed this massacre, which gave him the insight to defend the Palace with heavy artillery in 1795, leading to the turn of his fortunes.

experience and presented it to the British Society for Psychical Research.

Tuileries Palace and gardens

This is not the only such occurrence at the Tuileries reported to the British Society for Psychical Research. In May 1955, a London solicitor and his wife also encountered several 18th century figures in the garden.[27]

163 years spans the time from the initial sacking of the Tuileries to the 1955 incident with the London solicitor. The 1901 incident involving the Oxford professors occurred on the 2/3rds Mark. Of course, no one involved in these incidents would have known

---

[27] Talbot, Michael, The Holographic Universe, pp. 226-7, 1991 HarperCollins Publishers.

anything about the Synchronicity Code when their experiences took place.

What makes the Hugh Williams and Tuileries cases so interesting is that they deal with extreme coincidences and/or paranormal events that fall outside the bounds of our rational belief system. Many would doubt that these incidents even occurred. But now, *because events happened in accordance with the Synchronicity Code*, we have an independent form of validation that indeed the events happened as they were reported. No writer recounting these stories would have been aware that events across time often have the mathematical correlation claimed here. And yet the events have been mapped out exactly as the Synchronicity Code would lead us to expect.

The Titanic

Another case involves the sinking of the Titanic on April 14, 1912. The Titanic was on its maiden voyage, and was thought to be "unsinkable", yet it struck an iceberg at excessive speed and proved that to be very wrong. In part due to an insufficient number of lifeboats, over 1500 people died.

Fourteen years *earlier*, in 1898, Morgan Robertson published a novel about a ship named "Titan" which also sank in the Atlantic upon striking an iceberg. The Titan also had too few lifeboats. Then on December 19, 1997, very close to 100 years (Power of Ten) from when Morgan Robertson first published his novel, the movie Titanic was released, becoming one of the top grossing films of all time. Thus, two fictional works (the 1898 novel and the 1997 movie) are as bookends to the real sinking of the Titanic. I have not ascertained the exact date of publication of Robertson's novel, but if it was sometime early in 1898, then the interval between the novel and the actual sinking would roll forward 7 times to exactly the date of the movie's release.

Titanic at the docks.

Knowing as we now do of the Synchronicity Code's predilection for coincidences (paranormal or otherwise), we would look carefully at the Titanic for further clues to the unfolding of history. As it turns out, we are guided by another strange coincidence. An ocean liner stewardess named Violet Jessop was a survivor of *both* the sinking of the Titanic as well as the sinking of the Titanic's sister ship, the HMHS Britannic 1682 days later, on November 21, 1916.

How the Synchronicity Code maps this event is a little complex, but the correlation is striking. In actual fact, the Britannic was the *third* ship in the series to sink. If we take the interval between the sinkings of the Titanic and Britannic, 1682 days, and subtract it from the April 14, 1912 date (when the Titanic sunk), we get September 6, 1907. No ship sunk on that date. But *just one day later* the RMS Lusitania made its maiden voyage from Liverpool to New York City, on September 7th, 1907. This certainly "reminds" one of the maiden voyage that the Titanic was undertaking, from Southhampton to New York City.

Violet Jessop in her uniform
while assigned to *HMHS Britannic*

The Synchronicity Code link to the maiden voyage of the Lusitania is just the first part of this, however. For the Lusitania also sank at sea. Indeed, were it not for the Titanic movie, the Lusitania might have gone down in history as the most famous ship to have sunk during the 20th century, for on May 7, 1915, the RMS Lusitania was torpedoed by German U-boat U-20 and sank in 18 minutes. This sinking turned public opinion against

Germany and contributed to the United States entering the war on the side of the Allies.

Here's the final correlation. The sinking of the Lusitania occurred *a mere 3 days* from the exact 2/3^{rds} Mark (May 10, 1915) between April 14, 1912 (sinking of the Titanic) and November 21, 1916 (sinking of the Britannic).

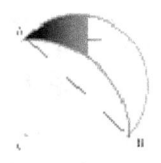

12

PREDICTING
THE
FUTURE

Prediction is very difficult, especially about the future.
Niels Bohr

If "history repeats" is the most oft-repeated adage about history, second place would go to "those who do not know history must repeat it"[28]. Just as we can't identify the underlying mechanisms at work in the Synchronicity Code, we can't be sure of the consequences of "time gnosis," in which there is public knowledge, in advance, of the timing of a possible future event. As of this writing we are staring at the possibility of major war and other crises right around the corner. By

---

[28] This phrase originated with George Santayana, who said, "Those who do not remember the past are condemned to repeat it."

shouting out some of these possibilities in advance, could the ill-effects be avoided or at least blunted?

Such is my hope.

Nothing validates the Synchronicity Code theory as much as the prediction of future events. However, it is not always so simple an affair as taking two dates and rolling them over to find the next event. There are a number of possible future dates that follow two meaningfully related predecessor dates utilizing the multiples and fractions described in Chapter 2. Two principles that can aid to narrow the choice of future dates are (i) when two timelines "triangulate", converging at a single future point in time, as introduced in Chapter 7, and (ii) the Power of Ten corollary.

A good example of how this could work would be to consider how things might have looked on the eve of World War I. We have shown how the starts of the Revolutionary War and Civil War precisely pointed via the Fibonacci ratio to the start of World War I. So you would have been on the alert starting in the Spring of 1914. But this particular Mark was just one of many possibilities, so you would not yet be convinced on this basis alone. Yet there were other indications based on the Synchronicity Code. The primary one was the Major War Cycle timeline itself, which was "due" to bring increased tensions reminiscent of the Battle of Leipzig 100 years earlier. Right here we have both triangulation (a converging, separate timeline) and Power of Ten strength. Another clue was that assassinations sometimes team up with the Major War Cycle, as they did with Lincoln. Thus the killing of Ferdinand was a warning sign— flashing red.

Before we get to the predictions, we need to lay the ground rules. The Chinese sage Lao Tzu said, "He who knows does not predict, he who predicts does not know." This can be understood in many ways, but the "knowing" of which Lao Tzu speaks would seem to relate to how future events may unfold, otherwise the saying doesn't make much sense. One can have an impression, a knowing of what may happen. But the approach needs to be accompanied by humility. Perhaps you know something yet always one remains in the midst of uncertainty. This strikes the right balance in approaching future events with respect to the Synchronicity Code. The Code does not "predict", but it does "know". It knows something about how patterns may unfold in the future (with more knowing possible as our understanding deepens), but it does not claim that a future event *must* occur at any particular place or time. Indeed, when a pattern seems most precise and perfect, one should expect the unexpected. Just because things unfold in accordance with an underlying order does not mean that that order cannot finally express with a great deal of variety.

Initial attempts at prediction

Synchronicity Code theory is just too new to have a lot of data about how it to anticipate future events using timeline projections. Nevertheless, since its discovery there have been a few opportunities to make a forecast, and see what follows. The results thus far have been promising.

The Versailles Cycle

My first official attempt at prediction went like this. As you read this, you will have little reason to doubt that this occurred, as the result was more fizzle than flash, but fascinating (and valid) nevertheless. In an email on May 19, 2009, I wrote:

"We are fast approaching a future event based on a Synchronicity Code sequence that started with the Treaty of Versailles. It is based upon the coincidence that World War 1 began on June 28, 1914 and ended on the exact 5-year anniversary of this date, June 28, 1919, when the Treaty of Versailles was signed.

"The event I am predicting is that a significant treaty or pact will be signed on the world stage within approximately 30 days of June 28, 2009. This has not happened every time (and on a couple of occasions it appears that major legislation stood in for "treaty") over the last 90 years, but it has happened often enough that we should look for it happening again now.

Other treaties or similar events in this timeline since the Treaty of Versailles include:

> *June 2, 1924   Coolidge signs Indian Citizen's Act of 1924. This is related to prior treaties with American Indians (most of which were broken).*

167

June 18, 1934 Indian Reorganization Act enacted.

May 22, 1939 Germany and Italy sign <u>Pact of Steel</u>.

July 22, 1944 <u>Bretton Woods agreements</u> establish International Banking Regulations and the IMF.

July 20, 1949 Israel and Syria sign <u>truce</u> ending 19 month war

June 21, 1954 <u>Geneva Conference</u> partitions Vietnam into North Vietnam and South Vietnam

July 2, 1964 Lyndon Johnson signs <u>Civil Rights Act of 1964</u>

June 18, 1979 Jimmy Carter and Leonid Brezhnev sign <u>SALT II</u> in Vienna

July 25, 1994 Israel and Jordan sign <u>peace treaty</u> ending state of war since 1948

June 9, 1999 Kosovo War: Yugoslavia and NATO sign <u>peace treaty</u>

June 28, 2004 <u>Sovereignty transferred</u> from U.S. to Iraq."[29]

---

[29] Ed. Note: text of email has been slightly edited.

The bull's eye for my upcoming prediction was June 28, 2009. Of course, virtually no one aside from me and a few others was aware that the Synchronicity Code was secretly at work. But as I was watching the news carefully, I found it: Iraq declared June 28, 2009 as a national holiday to mark the end of U.S. presence after more than 6 years of occupation, hailing the date *as a return to sovereignty*. Now look again at the last entry in the email, sent over a month earlier:

"*June 28, 2004 Sovereignty transferred from U.S. to Iraq.*"

The fact that this occurred exactly on the Versailles Cycle date is only part of why this counts as a success. The other part lies in the fact that exactly five years earlier the U.S. *purportedly* transferred sovereignty back to Iraq. But it was in name only. The real thing, from Iraq's perspective, required one more roll of the die. This wasn't the headline grabbing event I was looking for, but it was good enough for me.

So why the fizzle and not the flash?

It was fizzle because June 28, 2009 had none of the supporting factors that would have turned up the volume. Take a look at the list on the previous page and see where the big treaties, legislation or political act occurred. I would count the 1939 signing of the Pact of Steel, the Civil Rights Act, and Bretton Woods. 1939 was 25 years up from the start of the cycle, and since it is one-quarter of a century, it relates to the Power of Ten. The Civil Rights Act in 1964 was 50 years up—again the

Power of Ten. Bretton Woods was 30 years up—a Power of Ten number but not as significant as dates that multiply out to 100 years, as 1939 and 1964 did.

Where I *do* anticipate "flash" is right around the corner. The next cycle up is June 28, 2014, 100 years from the start of the Versailles Cycle. Whatever political act gets signed or agreed upon around this Mark will likely have far-reaching consequences. This also ties to the Major War Cycle, so watch carefully.

The 10-year Omigod Cycle

Time and tide wait for no man. (Author unknown)

My next attempt at prediction was set forth in an email dated July 20, 2009 and referenced a date that was looming in September. In looking back on it, I would not consider this to be a clear hit. But realize that this is perfectly allowed in these rolling type cycles. The reality is that sometimes they just don't happen. But the cycle could still be at work in the Marks to come. Here's what I wrote:

> *"Next up is a more explosive, more threatening cycle, the 10 Year Omigod Cycle*
>
> *September 3, 1929: U.S. Stock Market peak before the crash.*
>
> *September 1, 1939: Germany invades Poland, igniting WWII.*

August 29, 1949: USSR fires its first nuclear test weapon, igniting the Cold War.

Anyway, that's the start. Within 30 days of the Sept. 1 date, in most of these decadal increments, huge storms occur. So the prediction for 2009 is: (1) if a hurricane is bearing down somewhere during this period, EXPECT THE WORST from it; and (2) if a world event, financially, or militarily, happens around Sept. 1 (we may not know until after the fact), expect the event to have large ramifications.

Crowd gathers after stock market crash in October 1929

Later that day I further clarified my earlier email:

One axiom of the Synchronicity Code is "follow the coincidences". I looked at the start of WW2 and noticed that seminal events of 1929, 1939 and 1949 were very closely tied to the same calendar date. In effect, the sequence at work is the 10 year period, rolled over and over. We've seen this with the Pearl Harbor--9/11 cycle, the Versailles Treaty cycle, and now the "10-Year Omigod Cycle..

In looking at the rollovers of this Cycle, the first three—start of crash, start of ww2, start of cold war, are clearly man-made. Later dates are not necessarily so, but it appears that when there wasn't a clear man-made event, there tended to be MAJOR weather events. So that is the simple basis of the prediction.

To fill in the intervening dates:

1959: Typhoon Vera (Sept 26th)

1969: Hurricane Camille (most powerful in history to that date)

     Also: Sept 1: Libya coup brings Gaddafi to power
     Also: Sept 5 My Lai Massacre

1979: Hurricane Frederic (Sept 12) costliest to hit Gulf Coast up to that date

1989: Hurricane Hugo (Sept 21) $7 Billion in damage

1999: Izmit Earthquake (17 Aug) kills 17,000 and begins year long series of earthquakes.

2009: We'll see."[30]

Well, there was no calamitous man-made event in 2009. There were major weather events, although there wasn't one single mother-of-all-weather events. Here is what happened:

August 7: Typhoon Morakot hits Taiwan, killing 500.

September 26: Typhoon Ketsana causes record amounts of rainfall in Manila, leading to a declaration of a "state of calamity" in 25 provinces.

September 29: An 8.3 magnitude earthquake triggers a tsunami near the Samoan Islands, destroying many communities and killing at least 189. If I were to pick one event, that's the one. While the death toll was not as large as some natural disasters, this is more of a case of dodging a bullet. An 8.3 magnitude earthquake is huge, packing more force than all but 2 of the deadliest earthquakes in recorded history.

September 30: A 7.6 magnitude earthquake strikes off the coast of Sumatra, killing 1,000 in Indonesia. Notice

---

[30] Ed. Note: text of email has been slightly edited.

that this occurred right after the Samoan earthquake, with a large death toll. These likely qualify as hits.

Since making the Omigod Cycle prediction and watching what happened, I have become uncertain about whether the 1929-1939-1949 sequence continues to roll forward as I first concluded. The first three events in the series were all man-made and the Marks were hit very tightly. Subsequently, most of the Marks were hit by bad weather events and the dates were not nearly so precise. Furthermore, even though Vera, Camille, Frederic and Hugo were big hurricanes, they pale in comparison to Katrina, which did not fall on this cycle.

Should the 10-year Omigod Cycle prove to be in play, the next Mark is September 1, 2019. But 2029 would be a Power of Ten date, so that's the one where the magnitude of the unfolding events would be most significant.

The Surprise Attack Cycle Revisited

With respect to the Surprise Attack Cycle described in Chapter 9, since 9/11, one further projected Mark has come and gone and this one really worked. This date was March 27, 2010, which was within one day of the relevant event on March 26th. *This was the date that North Korea sank a South Korean ship by surprise torpedo attack.* Since then the region has been on high alert for the outbreak of war. As I watched events unfold, I did not know then, nor do I now, whether this attack would be recorded by history as the beginning of an eventual all out war between the two Koreas. We can safely say that the Synchronicity Code points to a real risk of war breaking out, but do not know if it will do so. While history repeats, it does not always do so with the same intensity. Since this incident immediately followed the 9/11 attack on a 60-year Power of Ten date, one might reason that this attack may not lead to devastating effects.

The next "surprise attack" is due October 10, 2018.

World War III

I've already laid out this particular projection in Chapter 9 so here will just repeat the timeline.

- **World War I begins** 1914
-
- 1/4 Mark: **World War II begins** 1939
-
-
-
-
-
-
- **World War 3 begins** Circa 2014

I reiterate that I am not *predicting* that this is going to happen, but I *know* that circa 2014 would be a clean hit of the Synchronicity Code *if* war breaks out. Should the timeline express in this way, my hope is that foreknowledge can help steer events on a safer course than would have been possible before the advent of the Synchronicity Code discovery.

Famine and Russian Winter

We stand in the shoes of Joseph who warned the Pharoah of seven years famine. While the famine could not be prevented, it could be prepared for, and its damaging consequences muted.

I uncovered a possible timeline involving famines while researching Napoleon's campaign in the Russian winter of 1812-3. The French losses had clear parallels to those of the Nazis in the winter of 1941-42. Two possible future time periods for military attrition in a similar Russian Winter are 2021-2 (1.618) and 2070-1. Neither future date expresses the Power of Ten corollary in its strongest form, although 2021 is 80 years up from the Nazi debacle. However, these dates are also connected to a famine timeline that may not directly relate to war.

Here are the key historical occurrences:

1601-3   This was the worst Russian famine, in terms of effect on the population, in which one third of all Russians died. It was due simply to severe cold weather.

1812-13 Hundreds of thousands of French soldiers die in Russian Winter.

1891-2 While cold weather was again a factor, inept and callous governmental handling of the food crisis played an important role, leading to the loss of half a million lives, and giving impetus to the Marxist movement.

1941-2 The Nazi invasion of Russia in Operation Barbarossa is considered one of the deadliest series of battles in the history of warfare.

First, see how triangulation of the above famine dates and Russian Winter war campaign dates pointed to the devastation of the Nazis.

1. 1891-1812 = 79. 79 x .618 = 49. 49 added to 1891 = 1940 (1941—Operation Barbarossa).

2. 1812-1601 = 211. 211 x .618 = 130. 130 added to 1812 = 1942 (1941—Operation Barbarossa).

Now take 1812 – 1601 = 211 again; 1812 + 211 = 2023, which is within one year of the 2021-2 winter cited above with respect to war attrition dates. Also, take the two war attrition dates of 1941-1812 = 129. 129 added to 1941 = 2070. Further, take 1891-1601 = 290 years. 290 years x .618 from 1891 = 2070. These both triangulate with the 2070 war attrition date shown above.

If you or happen to be in or around Russia, fill your grain bins starting around 2020, or earlier! Tell your progeny to fill them again prior to 2070.

The Space Shuttle Disasters

I include this one in the hope that a possible future event can be rendered untrue. Perhaps launches on future at-risk dates might be avoided, and just maybe reduce the threat to the safety of our astronauts (or other space travelers).

On January 28, 1986, the seven member crew of the Space Shuttle Challenger died 73 seconds into their flight due to failure of an O-ring seal. On February 1, 2003, the seven member crew of Space Shuttle Columbia met a similar fate upon re-entry into the Earth's atmosphere, due to damage to the thermal protection system from a piece of foam that detached during take-off. The coincidences of date (end of January/beginning of February), and number of crew, increase the likelihood of a 3rd future event in relation to the first two. Here are the next three future dates to watch out for, based on fractions and multiples of the 17 year time period between the 1986 and 2003 events:

July/Aug 2011 (17 x .5 = 8.5 years added to 2003= 2011)[31]

Jan/Feb 2014 (17 x .618 =10.5 years added to 2003= 2014)

Jan/Feb 2020 (2003 + 17 years)

---

[31] The final launch of Space Shuttle Atlantis is currently scheduled for early July 2011.

Jan/Feb 2037 (2003 + 17 + 17) this one totals 51, which is close to 50 years, so could have Power of Ten strength.

The Next Bill Gates

Both Bill Gates of Microsoft and Mark Zuckerberg, founder of Facebook, were Harvard drop-outs. Both started their companies when they were around 21 years old. Both have been criticized for their business tactics. Yet both are famous philanthropists. Both are also billionaires. That's a nice collection of coincidences to form the basis for a Synchronicity Code projection.

Bill Gates founded Microsoft on April 4, 1975, and registered the name "Microsoft" on November 26, 1976. If I were doing a detailed analysis and projection, I would keep track of both dates. But for our purposes here we will use the 1975 date.

Facebook was launched February 4, 2004. The number of days between the founding of Microsoft and launching of Facebook is 10,533, which is just shy of 29 years. The Synchronicity Code would project the following dates as ones to watch for the next Bill Gates or Mark Zuckerberg:

.25 (up from 2004): April 21, 2011 (just passed)

.33: August 11, 2013

.382: February 9, 2015

.5:   July 7, 2018

.618: November 20, 2021

.66: February 16, 2023

.75: September 21, 2025

1.0: December 6, 2032

I know; that's a lot of dates. I haven't attempted to narrow the field by triangulating the dates against any other timelines that might apply to these companies or their founders. However, there are also some Power of Ten possibilities, which would elevate certain dates in importance above the rest.

In this respect, the .382 date of February 9, 2015 is interesting in that it is very close to 40 years from the founding of Microsoft. Similarly, the .75 date of September 21, 2025 is 50 years from Microsoft's founding. Both dates reflect the Power of Ten (4 x 10 and 5 x 10). Especially if our next Bill Gates falls on the 50 year mark, we should expect great things, since that is a half-cycle of the more powerful 100 year cycle.

Even without first narrowing the choices, the above dates can be watched for signs of interesting new tech companies started by an Ivy League (especially Harvard) drop-out in his or her twenties. The parallel coincidences (Harvard, drop-out, etc.) are not mandatory, but they can provide clues as to the next huge tech star to appear.

As a projected Mark approaches, do not feel wedded to an exact date. If it hits within a month of the suggested date, I would consider that close enough to scrutinize any contender.

A Master Art Theft

It is the end of February 2011 as I write this. Last night I had what appears to have been an experience of synchronicity (the old-fashioned kind!) related to a Van Gogh masterpiece. Earlier in the day, my daughters went with their grandmother to the Museum of Modern Art and they were captivated by Van Gogh's Starry Night. In the evening I was doing some Synchronicity Code research unrelated to art when I accidentally come across a reference to Van Gogh's painting of this masterwork in 1889. Then this morning, the theme of art theft arose in my researches.

Van Gogh's Starry Night

I suppose that's all beside the point, if not for the fact that synchronicity is so significant to the subject I am writing about. Although this seems wildly unlikely, I think 2011 stands a chance to bear witness to a major art theft. Here's why.

On August 21, 1911, one century ago, Da Vinci's Mona Lisa was stolen from the Louvre in Paris by Vincenzo Peruggia. An Italian patriot, Peruggia's stated purpose (other than to line his own pockets) was to return the masterpiece to Italy to hang in a museum. The painting was recovered in Italy two years later, and Peruggia arrested, when Peruggia attempted to sell it to the directors of the Uffizi Gallery in Florence.

On August 21, 1961, Goya's portrait of the Duke of Wellington was stolen by an unemployed bus driver named Kempton Bunton shortly after the portrait was purchased by a wealthy American and displayed at the National Gallery. The thief gave up the painting in 1965, and since his motivation was apparently altruistic (he planned to give the ransom to the poor), he served only three months in jail.

No doubt you have noticed the coincidence that these two thefts each occurred on the calendar date of August 21st. Perhaps you also noticed that the two thefts were exactly 50 years apart, which is an expression of the Power of Ten. The rule of thumb is that where you see 50 years, think 100, as 100 reiterates the Power of Ten and is the strong case of it.

This is a set-up for an art theft of potentially major proportions in 2011, ideally (but not necessarily) on or about August 21st. The 2011 Mark could be realized in other ways that are meaningfully related to the first two, but we won't know until we get there. It is also possible that a meaningfully related event will in fact occur, but not be discovered until months or years later.

Triangulating with the above, though with less synchronicity, is a timeline projection based on the 1911 Mona Lisa theft and the theft of 20 Van Gogh paintings from the Stedelijk Museum in Amsterdam. This latter theft was perpetrated on April 14, 1991 by four Dutchmen. Fortunately the artwork was recovered very quickly, unfortunately with some damage to three of the pieces.

Here again we see the Power of Ten, in that 80 years separates the Van Gogh theft from the Mona Lisa. By projecting 20 years into the future, a presumed 2011 theft would fit neatly into a "roll back" from 1991 five times to the hundred year Mark in 1911. March 13, 2011 is the exact rollover date, but I am more persuaded by the coincidental August dates described above, and so would continue to look to late summer. A major art theft on any date in 2011 will qualify as a hit, but a precise hit would be in the third week in August.

What do the 1911, 1961 and 1991 events suggest about what may be about to unfold? Well, first, these thefts were all of masterpieces, so masterpieces are a fitting target. All three of the prior thefts were recovered, which hopefully would be the case here. One would think that the level of security today is higher than it has been in the past, which would seem to rule out a casual theft by an amateur thief, yet in the 1911 and 1961 cases, the thefts were by amateurs with at least some degree of altruistic intent. The 1991 Van Gogh thefts, however, did not fit this pattern.

As I write this the question arises again as to the effect of publicly announcing a possible art theft in advance of its occurrence. A thief might read this and try to fulfill the projection. Or security may be tightened which prevents a theft that would have otherwise occurred "in the dark". We just don't know.

A Superconductivity Breakthrough

This one has a little less going for it in terms of coincidence and triangulation, but it would still be very exciting if the prediction is realized. Superconductivity, which deals with zero electrical resistance in materials below a certain temperature, was discovered April 8, 1911 by Heike Kamerlingh Onnes, a well respected Dutch scientist who received the Nobel Prize for his work in 1913. Around April 17, 1986 (note the close correlation in calendar date) it was discovered that certain ceramic materials have critical temperatures above 90 K (-183 degrees Celsius). This breakthrough opened up prospects, potentially, for room-temperature superconductivity.

The 1986 date is important not only because it was a key milestone in the history of superconductivity, but also because it occurred very close to 75 years after the original discovery. This means that an event occurring at the Power of Ten 100 year anniversary of the original discovery by Kamerlingh Onnes would "roll back" from that 75 year Mark to that original discovery date in 1911.

That becomes our prediction, that something big will happen in the field of superconductivity research in 2011, with special focus on April 2011.

(Ed. Note: It is now at the end of March as this book is being prepared to go to press. On March 24, 2011, researchers at Stanford University in conjunction with the Department of Energy's SLAC National Accelerator Laboratory reported finding a "new phase of matter" as they researched a puzzling gap in electronic structures of some superconductive materials. Understanding this so-called "pseudo-gap" has been a 20-year scientific quest. I am not qualified to judge whether this breakthrough will be considered as a seminal breakthrough leading to eventual commercialization of room temperature superconductors. In any event, some time must pass before the scope of this discovery can be given historical context.)

Chinese Politics

China is such an important country these days that it cannot *not* be in the news. This prediction deals specifically with Chinese political fortunes, although the triggering event may be an uprising.

Within the last century, there have been three governing powers in China: (i) the imperial rule under

185

the Qing Dynasty, which form of government had lasted two thousand years until it ended following the Wuchang Uprising in 1911, (ii) the Republic of China, which was founded upon the collapse of imperial rule and continues to this day...in Taiwan, and (iii) the People's Republic of China, which was officially proclaimed by Mao Zedong upon communist victory in the Chinese civil war, in 1949.

The relevant Synchronicity Code calculation starts with the Wuchang Uprising on October 10, 1911 and multiplies the number of days between that date and October 1, 1949, which was the date the People's Republic was proclaimed, by the Fibonacci ratio 2.618. This gives March 13, 2011. Why this calculation? Because this particular Mark projects to the Power of Ten year of 2011, 100 years up from the 1911 uprising. The fact that both the 1911 and 1949 dates occurred in October also add some symmetry to the pairing and might be expected to "pull" the Mark from its exact Code multiplier to a date in October of 2011.

Late 2011, or perhaps early 2012 is also implicated by the November 7, 1931 declaration by Mao Zedong of the Chinese Soviet Republic, which is linked to the November 23, 1971 date in which the People's Republic of China took the Republic of China's (Taiwan) seat on the UN Security Council. These dates fall on the 20% and 61.8% Marks between 1911 and 2011; alternatively, if you rollover the interval between 1931 and 1971 you also hit the same 2011 point. So we have a triangulation to late 2011. December 9, 2011 is the exact rollover date, but November calendar date synchronicity could also be a factor.

As of this writing in late March 2011, at present there is nothing on the horizon that suggests how this all might unfold. Will history mark this by significant change in the relationship between the People's Republic of China and Taiwan? Will the People's Republic take a definitive step away from its Marxist/Communist ideology? Or will there be a major uprising?

The Wuchang Uprising is worth studying for parallels to how events may unfold. Back in 1911, the city of Wuchang was a manufacturing hub on the Yangtze River, producing military weapons for China's modernizing "New Army". Sun Yat-sen was at the center of events (even though he was in America at the time of the uprising). His revolutionary ideas, based on studies of Abraham Lincoln, Alexander Hamilton and philosopher Henry George, were at the heart of the revolutionary movement. Several officers of the New Army had secretly embraced Sun Yat-sen's ideology, which set the stage for the uprising. An accidental explosion led to a police investigation which uncovered the link between the military leadership and the revolutionaries. Facing arrest and execution, the military leaders boldly staged a coup. Acting quickly, they telegraphed the other provinces and asked them to declare their independence. The time was right, in part due to natural disasters (including a flood of the Yangtze River that killed 100,000) and within a matter of weeks, fifteen provinces had seceded. Underestimating the scope of events, the Qing Dynasty reacted slowly, which allowed the rebellion to take hold.   The Republic of China was declared by representatives from the seceding provinces within a month of the start of the uprising.

What struck me while researching this is that the technology of the time, the humble telegraph, allowed rapid coordination between provincial governments around the country. Today, cell phones and the internet allow even greater communication and coordination. Just how this will play out in mainland China, or in Taiwan, remains to be seen.

The Killing of Bin Laden

Like many Synchronicity Code sequences, the killing of Osama bin Laden, on May 1, 2011, both reflects into the past and points to the future. My nephew Oliver alerted me to the historical coincidence that bin Laden was killed within one day of the anniversary date of the day Hitler died, on April 30, 1945.   By following this date coincidence, we can calculate the following Code intervals between 1945 and 2011, which correlate with a number of important events at the interface of the Arab world and the West:

Start: April 30, 1945: Hitler dies

.2   July 12, 1958: On July 14, 1958, Arab nationalists overthrow the Iraqi government and King Faisal II is murdered.

.382 July 17, 1970: On July 23, 1970, Said bin Taimur, Sultan of Mercat and Oman is deposed in a palace coup by his own son Qabos.

.5 May 1, 1978: On April 27, 1978, Afghanistan President Daoud Khan is killed in a military coup.

.66 April 29, 1989: On June 3, 1989, Ayatollah Khomeini, leader of the 1979 Iranian Revolution, dies.

End: May 1, 2011: Osama bin Laden dies

Khomeini's death helps to unravel the link between Hitler and bin Laden. Both Hitler and bin Laden were fanatical, charismatic, and managed to grossly distort religious views to evil ends. Each of Hitler, Khomeini and bin Laden were intensely anti-semitic and anti-U.S.

The Hitler-bin Laden connection may have predictive significance out into the future. Any of the following dates could mark the death of another Arab or possibly anti-semitic, charismatic, fanatic-leader:

1.2 July 12, 2024

1.25 October 30, 2027

1.382 July 16, 2036

1.33 February 9, 2033

1.5 April 30, 2044

This last date, April 30, 2044 is the most harmonic because it is close to the 100 year mark of the death of Hitler, and also falls exactly on the anniversary date of Hitler's death.

Predicting the End of the World

As a wise mentor of mine once humorously put it, predictions of the end of the world create a problem. If we know the exact day, but not the exact time, what to do? If it hasn't happened by bedtime do we stay up for it or try to get a couple of winks so we're fresh for our trip to the hereafter? Then should we sleep in, or greet the destruction of the world with our favorite cup of coffee?

Specific dates have been predicted for the end of the world since, well, the beginning of the world. Thus far none have been right. I am skeptical that anyone can predict the end of humankind on planet earth to the specific day, month or year.

Nevertheless, I took a look to see if the current breathless anticipation of the Mayan end date of December 21, 2012 correlates with any obvious Synchronicity Code sequence. I can't say that none exist, but nothing obvious jumped out at me.

This being said, the 2012 date may correlate with a known long-term weather cycle related to ice ages. From a long-term point of view, the Earth is more often cold than not. Long periods of cold called glacial periods or ice ages are punctuated with shorter interglacial periods of warmer average global temperatures. We are currently in one such warmer interglacial period and have been throughout the march of civilization from pre-recorded history until now.

While the presumed duration of the current interglacial period is the subject of scientific debate, some reputable scientists argue that we now stand at the cusp where the next ice age could begin *any day*. That might be ok if it took thousands of years to get cold again. But the troubling thing is that current scientific evidence suggests that the onset of substantial glaciation is *abrupt,* perhaps even in a matter of a decade or two.

Ice age cycles are believed to relate to long term variations in the Earth's orbit around the sun. It is possible that the Mayans, experts in observing the heavens, were marking the beginning of the end of the current interglacial period.

But no, I don't think the world will end on December 21, 2012.

A Great Sage will be born circa 2280!

In Chapter 1, we presented evidence of the Great Sage Cycle involving Buddha, Pythagoras, Christ, Mohammed, so we will end with the dates farthest out into the future, as they are the future of Mankind. First, to recall the sequence:

Birthdates: Pythagoras - Jesus Christ - Mohammed

- Circa 570 BC <u>Both</u> **the Buddha and Pythagoras** are born
-
-
-
-
-
- 1/2 Mark: Circa 4 BC **Jesus Christ** is born
-
-
-
-
-
- Circa 571 AD **Mohammed** is born

Who came next? You may or may not know of the philosophers and sages that came after Mohammed in the following list, but they were truly among the most distinguished of their day, which makes the overall list rather extraordinary. It is also fascinating to see the pattern unfold in accordance with the spirit of the age. Adding 570 years to each prior date:

570 BC Buddha, Pythagoras

0 AD Jesus Christ

571 (+1) AD Mohammed

1138 AD (-2) Maimonides

1711 AD (+1) David Hume

1712 AD (+2) Jean-Jacques Rousseau

2280 AD A Great Sage will be born!

Of course, two more cycles up and you hit the year 3420 AD, which when added to the 570 BC years gives you a total of 3990 years. Given the time scale, I think we could call that one 4000 years, a Power of Ten Mark. That's a sage to *really* watch for!

13

PONDERING
THE MEANING
OF
THE SYNCHRONICITY CODE

"Let no one ignorant of geometry enter." On the doors
of Plato's Academy

This won't be easy. I have cast about for some
theory, some concept that helps us come to grips with the
meaning of the Synchronicity Code. The closest thing is
actually the source of my discovery: cycle theories used
in forecasting the markets. But I don't think this analogy
goes quite far enough. The Synchronicity Code embodies
principles of time and number that were envisioned by
the philosophers of the ancient world, the Greeks in
particular.

The "old master" of market prediction, R.N. Elliott, who originated Elliott Wave Theory, claimed that price changes in the stock market simply express the way things unfold in nature. Elliott based his method exclusively on the Fibonacci ratio, which while important, is not the sole approach taken here.

Scientists can and have explained why the Fibonacci ratio is indeed a natural one for things to grow by. But it one's thing to say that a conch shell takes the form of a logarithmic spiral based on the Fibonacci ratio. It is another thing to say that this mathematical constant is the cause of market patterns, let alone events of history, unfolding over the centuries. I think we need ancient Greek number theory to help bridge this conceptual gap.

The other "old master" market forecaster, W.D. Gann, had his own number cycles, which were closely aligned with the calendar year and utilized the Power of Ten. Gann also researched astrology (as did Jung, by the way), although his number cycles were not necessarily dependent on it. Perhaps they withheld their best secrets, but neither Gann nor Elliott's approaches, as handed down by them, make the prediction of market cycles a certainty. Some would therefore claim that their theories are untrue. I disagree. There is *something* to them. The question is how to understand that something.

One thing that I find interesting is that at one point, Robert Prechter, the pre-eminent disciple of Elliott and practitioner of Elliott Wave Theory, at one time was so successful that his forecasts would actually cause prices to move in the markets, sometimes dramatically.

However, the theory itself required that the crowds be wrong at the extremes, allowing one to "predict" that at some point Prechter would lose his market-ruling influence, which then happened due to a series of ill-timed calls. Why I find this interesting goes back to the notion of *time gnosis* which has been touched upon. What is the effect of knowing a Synchronicity Code sequence is due to be fulfilled, and even more to the point, what would be the effect if thousands of people know it? Does the Synchronicity Code work the same way when people know about it and can respond to it even before the event has occurred? To me, this is the big question.

The Tetractys

There is something about the ancient Greeks. They were the ones that said "all is arranged according to number." Egyptian and Babylonian priests may have said it first, but the ancient Greeks announced it to the world. They didn't mean this in the modern sense of measurements and statistics. They meant that number is *qualitatively* implicit in life itself. That is exactly what the Synchronicity Code seems to validate. The Greeks envisioned all of life as geometrically flowing from a single source of eternal Being into the various forms seen on earth. A sacred symbol for this, to the Pythagoreans, was the Tetractys, which is an equilateral triangle formed out of the first ten points aligned in four rows:

•

• •

• • •

• • • •

The Pythagorean Tetractys

The Tetractys offers an image with which to ponder the Synchronicity Code. First, Pythagoras held that everything had three component parts to it, which is symbolized by the three corners of the symbol. In the Synchronicity Code, time is always separated out into at least three events: two events that are used to measure the span across time, and a third event that is the Mark (whether occurring between the first two points in time, before or after). Also, the outer lines of the triangle converge at 3 points, depicting the practice of triangulating converging timelines. Finally, for Pythagoras, ten is a sacred number, and is symbolized by the ten points that make up the Tetractys on four rows. In the Synchronicity Code, the Power of Ten has been found to be an important component of how events unfold across time.

Eternal Recurrence

The Synchronicity Code embraces a cyclical conception of time, which is in harmony with the views held in antiquity by the Pythagoreans, as well as by the ancient Egyptians, Indians, Mayans, Chinese, really *all* of the ancient philosophical and spiritual traditions. In more recent times, Nietsche, Ouspensky and others have taken this view one step further and explored the theory of eternal recurrence, in which life as we live it will occur over and over again *exactly as we are now living it.*

A close family friend comes from a family where it is generally acknowledged (but rarely talked about) that mothers and grandmothers down through the generations frequently have psychic abilities. She firmly believes in the notion of eternal recurrence, based on the fact that she periodically dreams future events with movie-like exactitude, only to experience the same scenes months later.

From a theoretical point of view, the theory of recurrence stems from the mathematical premise that, since the probability of our world existing exactly as it does is finite, yet time and space are infinite, then it is a mathematical necessity that our present existence will recur an infinite number of times.

I'm not sure this works for me. For one thing, the formulation doesn't seem to preclude infinite *other* lifetimes, besides the one I am living now. For another, the Synchronicity Code suggests that it is meaning, and not the very same persons and events, that repeats. Finally, fixed eternal recurrence precludes free will, and free will is *more interesting* than not having any. Without interest, life withers and dies.

While I am not sure I can give an adequate answer to what the Synchronicity Code is or what it means, I can offer the following ponderings as to its meaning and significance.

A.   If the lives of Jefferson and Adams, or Lincoln and Kennedy, are mathematically linked across the centuries, and at the same time the wars they started or ended are also linked together, and at the same time their wives and children are integrally connected to them across the fields of time (so they could show up on cue just when they are supposed to), all as the Synchronicity Code suggests, then *life itself is probably something altogether different than we imagined.* It begins to look like ONE THING. One Being. One living, breathing life-force in which all its parts are geometrically related in time and space, like a perfect diamond.

B.   History may repeat via recurrence or reincarnation of souls, I don't know. The Synchronicity Code suggests that what repeats is the *meaning* of an event. That meaning could be an invention, an assassination, a world war, the birth of sages, or the birth of your own child. But each turn is a little different from the last, which may be the opening for free will.

C.   Sometimes the meaning of events is more energetic, like the energy of a bad storm, than thematic.   That is how I see the relationship between the start of the 1929 crash, the beginning

199

of World War II in 1939 and the first Soviet atomic bomb explosion in 1949.

D.   The Synchronicity Code freely trades beginnings and endings in its expressions of meaning.   Abraham Lincoln was assassinated at the end of the Civil War, and Franz Ferdinand at the beginning of World War I. But both men share the assassination and war timelines of which they were a part.

E.   The <u>con</u>currence of two meaningfully-related events in one moment is what is usually meant by Jung's term "synchronicity". The Synchronicity Code deals with the <u>re</u>currence of meaningfully-related events over specific intervals of time. In either case, a fundamental building block of individual and collective history, and thus ourselves, is "meaning".   Since it requires an intelligent being to perceive that meaning, this raises the philosophical question as to whether the trees of human history make a sound when they fall if no one is around to hear them.

F.   While   synchronicity   is   sometimes dismissed as unscientific, perhaps due to its "just so", non-repeating nature, the Synchronicity Code may move the line a bit toward scientific verifiability.   When three (or more) events are synchronistically linked across time, it makes the accompanying meaningfully-related coincidences that much more improbable as pure chance.

G.　The Synchronicity Code may offer a theoretical explanation for why, in some instances, meaningful coincidences occur in the first place. They are occurring because the meaning of the events are historically repeating.　Thus, it is not just chance that both Lincoln and Kennedy were seated next to their wives, that both men were shot in the head, that both had vice presidents named Johnson succeed them, that Andrew Johnson was born in 1808 and Lyndon Johnson in 1908, that John Wilkes Booth was born in 1839 and Lee Harvey Oswald in 1939, and that both assassins were Southerners in their twenties.　These are amazing coincidences.　But perhaps they arise in the first place as by-products of the underlying force that is correlating events across time.

H.　I don't think the Synchronicity Code implies predestination.　While some huge events across time may have such power behind them that the projected event is likely to occur no matter what, this doesn't mean that individuals have no free will.　As one example, while the births of my children and their mother are synchronistically linked across forty years, this does not mean that myriad choices aren't exercised every day as their lives are lived out.

I.　For the same reason (that there is still plenty of room for free will), even if the Synchronicity Code forecasts the timing of a future event, there remains a vast array of possibility as to how that event will play out.

201

Again, as of this writing, we still don't know whether the North Korean torpedo attack on South Korea will eventually be seen as the first act of a new war. The event occurred right on schedule under the surprise attack cycle, but the magnitude of the event can't be known with certainty.

J.   Because the magnitude of events is not known with certainty, herein lies the greatest hope that I could have for the Synchronicity Code. The hope is that adverse future events can be prevented, or at least blunted, because they were *known* before the event occurred. The new axiom would be, that he who does not know *how history is repeating* must repeat it.

K.   Stated somewhat differently, the good timelines will take care of themselves. But with respect to future correlations of an ominous nature, shouting from the rooftops may be just what is required, for a large a public awareness could potentially mollify the adverse effects of the timeline that bears down upon us.

Is this even possible?

Only time will tell.

POSTSCRIPT

To choose time is to save time. Francis Bacon

The experience of discovering, researching and writing about the Synchronicity Code has been at once both miraculous and unsettling. In particular, I have not enjoyed facing the dark side of events that are mapped by the Synchronicity Code. But I think I've found a constructive vantage point and perspective.

When destructive patterns are revealed, those of assassinations, wars, natural disasters and the like, some solace is given by the very fact that these events are taking place according to a larger order implied by the Synchronicity Code. This doesn't mean that these events are "divinely inspired" or even "good", but they may be largely inevitable, and a part of a higher order of things that we can only guess about.

While the Synchronicity Code carries some suggestion that events are pre-destined, I myself do not hold this view. Regardless of the magnitude events, it seems to me that the possibility exists to deal with the future in constructive ways: to steer clear of adversity if possible, but if not, to prepare for it, and seek out opportunities to lessen the adverse consequences. Right now, it remains to be seen that foreknowledge of events can make a difference in their outcome.

As a final word, the meaning of the Synchronicity Code is both profound and ultimately uplifting, for I can find no concept or model that explains it other than that...

... *all life is One.*

The End

J. Andrew Goodman
June 21, 2011

ABOUT THE AUTHOR

Mr. Goodman graduated Summa Cum Laude from Bucknell University in 1981, graduating first in his class (B.A. Philosophy), and Columbia Law School in 1985. He is a practicing lawyer, an active investor, enjoys musical improvisation, and is a lifelong student of the great spiritual traditions. Mr. Goodman lives in northern Westchester, New York with his wife and three children.